The Outreach and Membership Idea Book Volume III

URJ-CCAR Commission on Outreach and Membership

URJ Press
New York, New York

This book is dedicated to the memory of
Mel Merians, *z"l*, first chairperson of the Task Force on the Unaffiliated
and chairperson of the Commission on Reform Jewish Outreach,
whose passionate commitment to welcoming the stranger
and to *keiruv*, bringing near those who are far from our community,
helped empower Reform congregations to open their doors
even wider to those seeking entry.

"Mel's commitment to Outreach never wavered—not for a minute. It was his great passion.
Mel was one of Reform Judaism's great Outreach pioneers;
like so much else in his life, he pursued this ideal with fierce intensity and zest,
and here, too, our Movement will forever be in his debt.
His z'chut—that is, his merit, his influence, his memory—
they hover over us, protect us, enlarge us, and give us strength."

Rabbi Eric H. Yoffie
President of the Union for Reform Judaism

Every attempt has been made to obtain permission to reprint previously
published material. The publisher gratefully acknowledges the following
for permission to reprint previously published material:

DR. CHRISTINA AGER: "From Chametz to Rosh Hashanah," used by permission.

THE BALTIMORE SUN: F. Kay, Liz. "High Holy Days Head Outside: Casual Worship
Part of Jewish Outreach." *The Baltimore Sun*, 12 Sept. 2007.

Copyright © 2010 by URJ Press
Manufactured in the United States of America
This book is printed on acid-free paper.
10 9 8 7 6 5 4 3 2 1

2009 URJ-CCAR Commission of Outreach and Membership

Judy Berg, *Chairperson*
Rabbi Stephen J. Einstein, *Co-Chairperson*
Dr. Peter Adland, *Vice-Chairperson*
Rabbi Howard Jaffe, *Vice-Chairperson*

Kathryn Kahn, *Executive Editor*
Vicky Farhi, *Editor*

David Aaronson
Dr. Marcia Abraham*
Sandra V. Abramson
Rabbi Larry Bach
Rabbi Morris Barzilai
Rabbi Marc Berkson
Anne Berman-Waldorf
Austin Beutel
Rabbi Aaron Bisno
Rabbi Eric Bram
Judy Bricker
Rabbi Barry Cohen
Rabbi Jordan Cohen
Paul Cohen
Sarah Cohen
Cantor Don Croll
Kathy Decker
Georgia DeYoung
Rabbi Michael Dolgin
Rabbi David Ellenson**
Catherine Fischer

Rabbi Steven Foster*
Rabbi Steven Fox**
Nancy Gennet
Rabbi James Gibson
Rabbi Arnold S. Gluck
Steve Goren
Barbara Gould
Art Grand
Janice Gutfreund
Rabbi Debbie Hachen
Rabbi Stephen Hart
Rabbi Geoffrey Huntting
Rene Katersky
Jack Kugelmass
Rabbi Judy Lewis
Carole Lieberman
Rabbi Alan Litwak
Rabbi Rosalin Mandelberg
George Markley
John McNamara
Rabbi Jonathan Miller

Paula Milstein
Rabbi James Mirel
Rabbi Jeremy Morrison
Renee Nadel
David Oney
Myra Ostroff*
Dr. Robert Mike Rankin
Rabbi Larry Raphael
Cantor Jacqueline Rawiszer
Jane Rips
Jon Rosen
Ginny Rosenberg
Rabbi Mark Schiftan
Rhea Schindler*
Rabbi Susan Shankman
Rabbi Jeffrey Sirkman
Toni Smeltzer
Rabbi Andrew Vogel
Diane Weiner
Dr. Nancy Wiener
Rabbi Eric Yoffie**

* Lifetime Member
** Ex Officio

Outreach and Membership Consultants

Rabbi Victor Appell Outreach Specialist
Dr. Paula Brody Outreach Specialist
Arlene Chernow Outreach Specialist
Vicky Farhi Outreach Specialist
Kathy Kahn Membership Specialist

THE BELIN OUTREACH AND MEMBERSHIP AWARDS

This year marks the eighth presentation of the Belin Outreach and Membership Awards established by David Belin, *z"l*, the founding chairman of the Commission on Reform Jewish Outreach. These awards honor congregations for their exceptionally innovative, effective, and reproducible Outreach and Membership programs.

Special thanks to the professional staff and to the Outreach and Membership chairs and committees of the congregations who received Belin Outreach and Membership Awards, whose creative work appears here:

BELIN AWARDS

Baltimore Hebrew Congregation, Baltimore, MD
Congregation Beth Israel, San Diego, CA
Congregation B'nai Israel, Boca Raton, FL
Congregation Rodeph Shalom, Philadelphia, PA
Congregation Shalom, North Chelmsford, MA
Temple Beth El, Boca Raton, FL
Temple Emanu-El, Dallas, TX
Temple Hesed, Scranton, PA
Temple Israel, Memphis, TN

BELIN HONORABLE MENTIONS

Congregation Beth Am, Los Altos Hills, CA
Congregation Beth Torah, Overland Park, KS
Holy Blossom Temple, Toronto, CAN
Leo Baeck Temple, Los Angeles, CA
Ohef Sholom Temple, Norfolk, VA
Temple B'nai Israel, Oklahoma City, OK
Temple Shalom, Dallas, TX
Temple Sinai, Atlanta, GA

Contents

Foreword	**vii**
Chapter 1: Recruitment: Increasing Our Membership and Welcoming New Members into Our Congregations	**1**
Comprehensive Membership Initiative	3
Shalom Squad	25
Rosh Hashanah under the Stars	36
Whatever Happened to the Wandering Jews of Chelmsford?	46
Chapter 2: Integration and Retention: Creating Early and Ongoing Connections That Ensure Lifelong Membership	**55**
Community Connectors	57
Davening and Dining	72
Open Tent	75
Reach Out and Connect-a-thon	80
Chapter 3: Outreach: Helping All to Find Their Place in Jewish Life	**93**
Baderech (On the Path)	94
Celebrating Our Diversity	139
Integrating Basic Judaism Students into the Life of the Synagogue	154
Jewish Children of Interfaith Families	179
Chapter 4: College and 20s/30s: Nurturing Connections to Our Jewish Community	**183**
Sha'arei Shabbat	184
Community Six-Pack	189
Gesher (Bridge)	203
Chapter 5: Early Childhood: Connecting Young Families to Preschool and Congregation	**213**
Goodnight Shabbat	214
Little Blossoms	225

Foreword

The Outreach and Membership Idea Book, Volume III reflects the exceptional work that our Reform congregations are doing in the areas of Outreach and Membership. This book honors and reflects this excellence in programming, which touches the lives of young adults, interfaith couples and families, those who choose Judaism as adults, single adults, empty nesters, prospective and current temple members, non-Jewish parents who are raising Jewish children, and many, many others.

As in the previous volume, this book includes both traditional Outreach programs to interfaith couples and families and innovative programs that support those in the process of conversion. You will also find membership programs with a focus on reaching prospective and new members, reconnecting with present members, and making all into lifelong members! In addition, this book includes wonderful programs that model attracting and engaging college students, and programs that reach out to people in their twenties and thirties in your community. These groups now make up a large percentage of the Jewish community. Many young adults are unaffiliated but are looking for a home in your congregation.

We invite you to replicate these creative offerings in your own congregation, tailoring and modifying them to suit the needs of your membership. Should you have any questions about program content or logistics, we suggest you contact the congregations that authored them. You will find contact information for each program entry along with the program description. We extend our thanks to all the congregations that submitted their programs and that engage in the sacred work of Outreach and Membership every day, to the benefit of our Jewish community. And *yasher koach* to those congregations whose award-winning programs are included in *The Outreach and Membership Idea Book Volume III* for generously sharing their ideas and materials with us, and through this book, with all of our Reform synagogues across North America.

We would like to particularly thank our **Belin selection committee**, drawn from the URJ-CCAR Commission on Outreach and Membership and staffed by Assistant Director, Vicky Farhi. Rabbi Debbie Hachen, Rabbi Alan Litwak, Georgia DeYoung and Anne Berman Waldorf all dedicated many hours to reading the numerous entries and engaging in the difficult process of selecting the winning programs that appear in this volume.

Our Reform synagogues have committed themselves to the mitzvot of welcoming the stranger, opening their doors to those who wish to draw near, and creating a culture of lifelong membership. As we celebrate three decades of this important work, we look forward to the next thirty years of outstanding Outreach and Membership programming.

Judy Berg, Chair
Rabbi Stephen J. Einstein, Co-chair
URJ-CCAR Commission on Outreach and Membership

Chapter One

Recruitment: Increasing Our Membership and Welcoming New Members into Our Congregations

Attracting and welcoming potential members is vital to every congregation. How to find them and connect in a way that makes them want to learn about your congregation is often a challenge.

For the first time in its history, Temple Hesed developed an aggressive **Comprehensive Membership Initiative** to seek out and reach unaffiliated Jews and interfaith families in northeastern Pennsylvania. The temple accomplished this by increasing its visibility, highlighting the diversity of its members, demonstrating a welcoming attitude toward interfaith families, and inviting local college students for Shabbat dinner. The efforts were a success, with a notable increase in temple membership and visibility in the community.

Often, potential members don't see the synagogue as a place for them. Baltimore Hebrew Congregation wanted all to see how welcoming it was, so it held its Erev Rosh Hashanah family service at a local park and invited everyone! Advertising it to the public as **Rosh Hashanah under the Stars**, the first year brought over 2,000 people, the second year 3,400! The congregations welcomed the affiliated and unaffiliated, interfaith families, couples, seniors, empty nesters, young families, and young adults. Baltimore Hebrew Congregation has increased its membership, but even more importantly, it has increased its visibility and reputation for being a welcoming community.

Congregation Beth Torah's congregational goal was to create sacred community before, during, and after worship! The **Shalom Squad** elevated the position of usher to one of honor in the synagogue. Each member of the Shalom Squad focused on greeting, offering hospitality, and providing friendly attentiveness before, during, and after worship to all who entered the building. Through careful training, each member of the Squad was able to make a positive impact on members and increase the welcome of the worship experience.

How do you give a voice to those who founded your synagogue while acknowledging the contributions of newer members? Congregation Shalom found a unique way to celebrate its fortieth anniversary, honor founding and long-time members, and welcome new members.

Whatever Happened to the Wandering Jews of Chelmsford? is a video given to current and potential members that tells the story of the congregation from its inception until today. The stories of founding members and the different stages of the synagogue's growth are linked to the congregation's future. Newer members of Congregation Shalom get a greater understanding of where Congregation Shalom has come from and perhaps gain a clearer sense of its direction for the future.

Comprehensive Membership Initiative

Congregation:	Temple Hesed
Address:	1 Knox Road, Scranton, PA 18505
Phone number:	570-344-7201
Contact's Name and E-mail:	Marilyn Deutsch, mhdeut@epix.net
Number of Member Units:	193
URJ District:	East District
Rabbis:	Rabbi Daniel J. Swartz
Membership Chair:	Marilyn W. Deutsch, Ph.D.

Brief Description: For the first time in Temple Hesed's nearly 150-year history, we have developed an aggressive, multifaceted membership initiative to seek out and welcome unaffiliated Jews and interfaith families. This is also the first time any synagogue in Scranton has explicitly targeted interfaith families in its programming.

Program Goals: Our overall goal was to reach out to unaffiliated Jews in northeastern Pennsylvania by increasing the visibility of our temple, highlighting the diversity of its members, and demonstrating our welcoming attitude toward interfaith families.

Target Population: Unaffiliated Jews in northeastern Pennsylvania, interfaith families, GLBT community.

Staffing Required: Rabbi and eight members of the Membership/Outreach Committee.

Total Cost of Program: $2,500 (includes Outreach materials, publicity, survey mailings).

Source of Funding: Taste of Judaism grant, targeted congregational donations, Oppenheim Institute.

Logistics: We implemented the following strategic plan:

1. *Establishment of a Membership/Outreach Committee* We established a diverse membership committee composed of individuals of all ages and all family compositions, who were personally involved in or had an interest in supporting interfaith marriages, same sex marriages, and/or interracial marriages. In addition to our seven-member, *active* membership committee, we also have five additional outreach "point people," one at our local medical school and each of four local colleges in our community.

2. *Development of Membership/Outreach Materials* We developed a membership brochure that highlights interfaith activities and shows how our temple is a "*Welcoming community, open and accepting of all those in search of a spiritual and social home . . . and welcomes individuals of all 'lifestyles.'*" In our brochure we highlight pictures of interfaith families who have leadership positions in our temple. This brochure is disseminated in libraries, hotels, the chamber of commerce, academic institutions, and community centers. It, along with brochures such as *Intermarried? Reform Judaism Welcomes You*, *Becoming a Jew*, *What's Missing From Our Congregation? You!*, and fact sheets developed by URJ—which we purchased this year—are available at all times at the

4   The Outreach and Membership Idea Book Volume III

temple, and when possible at every public event associated with Temple Hesed. (Please see attached brochure.)

Working with the URJ Web-Builder team, we also developed Temple Hesed's first dedicated website, www.templehesed.org, which clearly highlights our interfaith activities. (Previously, we had been a part of the local Federation's website.) We also developed a new membership/informational booklet and packet to send in response to all membership inquiries. The booklet highlights how we welcome interfaith families.

3. *Educational Outreach*

   a. We received a grant from the Union for Reform Judaism to advertise in secular newspapers and to conduct our first Taste of Judaism Class. Of the twenty-five participants, five expressed an interest in conversion, and three of them have already started classes with our rabbi. One unaffiliated Jew joined our temple before the class was completed and is now one of our most active sisterhood members! In addition to the educational format developed by URJ, we had Temple Hesed volunteers provide ethnic foods, which involved congregants in the process, gave a sense of warmth to the class, and introduced participants to Jewish foods and customs.

   b. Through our Oppenheim Institute Social Action Program, we addressed issues that impact individuals of all religions, encouraging interfaith couples and families to participate. Speakers included Rev. Barry Lynn, who spoke of separation of church and state; ACLU attorneys, who spoke about Evolution and Intelligent Design; Rabbi David Saperstein, who spoke on the confluence of religion and politics in the 2008 election; the president of a local college (non-Jewish), who spoke about the United Nations; and most recently, a documentary filmmaker, who spoke on pollutants in our environment.

   c. We are blessed that a member of one of the interfaith families that joined the temple as a result of an Oppenheim Institute Social Action Program is a retired newspaper and TV reporter. Under his direction, our rabbi now has a monthly op-ed column in the local paper addressing interfaith issues. Temple programs with an interfaith appeal have been widely covered in the local papers and TV news programs. Most recently, our "Blessing of the Sun" service was highlighted on the morning news program watched by 80 percent of local morning viewers.

4. *Engagement of Temple Leadership in Membership, Outreach and Retention*   To assure that all leadership were in agreement and supported the membership committee's objectives, including reaching out to new members, we chose to forego traditional board meetings and board reports so that we could have two board meetings during the past year dedicated entirely to

   a. *Interfaith Issues*   This allowed us to meet the following goal: *To provide a level of comfort for interfaith families by clarifying policies at Temple Hesed.* Outcomes from the board meeting included:

      • A proposed task force on interfaith members, to be led by a board member who is in a leadership position and currently in an interfaith marriage.

      • A weekly ad in the religious section of a local newspaper that never had synagogue representation. We asked for the logo to be changed to include a Star of David, and we write on each ad, "Interfaith families welcome."

      • We also disseminated URJ's *A Two-Year Action Plan for Your Congregation to Recognize and Honor Non-Jews Raising Jewish Children and to Invite and Support Conversion, Intermarried? Reform Judaism Welcomes You*, and *18+ Ways to Welcome and Support Interfaith Families*, as a guide for all board members and present congregants, and we have these brochures available at all times.

b. *Membership Recruitment and Retention* Our temple board approved a free introductory membership, which has been extremely well received by young interfaith couples without children. We entitle it "Try Us, You'll Like Us!" To date, 90 percent of families given free membership have chosen to remain as dues-paying members.

- All new members were welcomed by having their picture and an article about them in our monthly newsletter.
- New members were given a volunteer form and invited to various committee meetings by committee chairs.
- New members were given free admission to all events and a personal phone invitation by a member of the event committee asking if they wanted to go together.
- All new members were given a Hesed, Challah, and Honey bag at the High Holidays, which was brought to their house by a member of Sisterhood.
- All new members were invited to a Shabbat dinner at the temple with the board of directors and, at another time of the year, to a casual brunch.
- All new members were provided with a year's free membership to Sisterhood with a Sisterhood member calling them to ask if they would like to share a ride to an event.
- All new members were given honors at High Holy Days and/or invited to walk behind the Torah.
- All new members were asked to fill out a membership survey after one year. It was accompanied by a letter asking, "How are we doing?"

During the board meeting dedicated to membership recruitment and retention, we recognized those board members who had brought in new members, and we asked each board member to take an active role in connecting them to our community.

- Host a new member by calling them and asking them to come to services, join with them in a Shabbat dinner, or accompany them to an event.
- Call current but inactive members to ask them to join them for a temple activity.

Evaluation of Program: The membership committee, on behalf of the board, also sent out a membership survey and exit survey to assess satisfaction or dissatisfaction with the congregation.

Follow-up: We actively addressed all areas of dissatisfaction and had a plan of correction that we disseminated in a newsletter. The membership chair called all members who had resigned and completed the exit survey, told them the plan of correction, and if they were members in good standing, invited them back to the congregation.

Solidifying the Temple Hesed Community

Membership Committee Temple Hesed
April, 2008

As a member of the board of directors, chairperson of a committee, project or event, we realize that it is sometimes more efficient in the short term to do things by yourself or call on your friends, family or people with whom you are most familiar with to get the job done. However, to help us achieve our long term goals of strengthening our congregation, part of our leadership role is to assure that EVERY Temple Hesed congregant who walks through our doors feels welcome, valued, and included. To achieve our goals, we are asking you to do the following:

Please review our updated membership list. You will note that in the back of the list, we have a listing of individuals and families who have joined Temple Hesed during the past few years. We also have a listing of our major committees, and the individuals who serve on those committees. We also have an active volunteer list (consisting of those members who took the time to complete the form.

Please note that we have names of all family members on the membership list. Therefore, as you are "reaching out" to others, make a mental note of whether or not they are already involved on other committees or the board. If they are not.....then consider the following:

1. Please reach out to your old acquaintances who are not actively involved in Temple at this time.

    a. Give them a call and ask how they are.

    b. Ask them to join you for dinner and services, or to attend a Temple event with you.

    c. Ask them to participate with you on a committee, or do ONE TASK to help with a Temple event. If it is a Temple event, ***Please start small***. Most people love to get involved if they feel it is a time limited task that may be fun for them to do. Find out their comfort zone and work to find a place for that person. It may be helpful to ask with which three things they would prefer to help.

    d. See if they need a ride to an event.

2. Please reach out to new members.

    a. Call them and introduce yourself.

    b. Ask if they would be interested in having you accompany them to an event or service. Make sure you sit with them and introduce them to others.

    c. Find out their interests and try to pair them up with members with similar interests.

    d. Try to fill up your volunteers for events by mixing the regulars with the new members and the less active members.

If someone volunteers to help, FIND THEM A JOB, no matter how small.

Welcome Letter

Thank you for your interest in membership at Temple Hesed of Scranton. Hesed means loving kindness, and that is our approach to membership. Each application is handled individually to assure that all interested individuals can become a part of our Hesed Family. Once you have received this packet, please expect a call from a member of our membership committee within two weeks.

Completing and returning the enclosed Hesed Welcome Form will enroll you as an introductory member in our Temple. We are proud of our diverse congregation, varied programs, and comprehensive service designed to meet the needs of members of all ages and interests. We are a small Temple, which allows us to support and care for each other's needs, and to enjoy and celebrate each member's joyful occasions. We extend a warm welcome to new members as they find their niche in our many activities, including involvement with the greater Jewish community of Northeastern Pennsylvania.

Our membership committee is comprised of volunteers. We try to "match" you with a Hesed Host, a congregant who may, if you desire, host you and introduce you to the Temple Hesed family. If for some reason you are not called within two weeks after receiving this application and completing the Welcome Form, please contact the Temple office at 344-7201, or via email at templehesed@verizon.net so that we can make sure to follow up.

Looking forward to having you join our Temple Hesed Family.

In Hesed,

Rabbi Daniel Swartz Mark Davis
Spiritual Leader President

MEMBERSHIP

Temple Hesed

1 Knox Road • Scranton, PA 18505

phone: (570) 344-7201 • fax: (570) 344-4514

www.templehesed.org • templehesed@verizon.net

ADULT APPLICANT #1

NAME _____ GENDER (circle) M F
        Mr./Dr./Mrs./Ms./Hon.   Last   First   Middle

MARITAL STATUS (circle) Single Married (date)___/___/___ Divorced Separated BIRTH DATE ___/___/___

HOME ADDRESS _____
            Street   City   State   Zip

PHONE NUMBER _____
            Home Phone   Business Phone   Mobile Phone

E-MAIL ADDRESS _____
            Primary   Business/Secondary

OCCUPATION _____

Chapter One   Recruitment   **9**

Position/Title   Company

BUSINESS/SECONDARY ADDRESS

_____

Street   City   State   Zip

RELIGIOUS BACKGROUND ☐ Reform ☐ Other Jewish ☐ Not Jewish ☐ Bar/Bat Mitzvah ☐ Confirmation

ADULT APPLICANT #2

NAME _____ GENDER (circle) M F

Mr./Dr./Mrs./Ms./Hon.   Last   First   Middle

MARITAL STATUS (circle) Single Married (date)____/____/____ Divorced Separated BIRTH DATE ____/____/____

HOME ADDRESS

_____

Street   City   State   Zip

PHONE NUMBER _____

Home Phone   Business Phone   Mobile Phone

E-MAIL ADDRESS _____

Primary   Business/Secondary

OCCUPATION _____

Position/Title   Company

The Outreach and Membership Idea Book Volume III

BUSINESS/SECONDARY ADDRESS

_____

| | Street | City | State | Zip |

RELIGIOUS BACKGROUND ☐ Reform ☐ Other Jewish ☐ Not Jewish ☐ Bar/Bat Mitzvah ☐ Confirmation

CHILDREN (use "Additional Info" for more children)

#1   NAME

_____

| | Last | First | Middle | Hebrew |

GENDER (circle) M F BIRTH DATE ___/___/___ GRADE ___ E-MAIL ADDRESS_____

MARRIED (circle) N Y If yes, Spouse's Name _____ Grandchildren's Names _____

ADDRESS (if not living at home/at college) _____

| | Street | City | State | Zip |

#2   NAME

_____

Last   First   Middle   Hebrew

GENDER (circle) M F BIRTH DATE ___/___/___ GRADE ___ E-MAIL ADDRESS_____

MARRIED (circle) N Y If yes, Spouse's Name _____ Grandchildren's Names _____

ADDRESS (if not living at home) _____

| | Street | City | State | Zip |

#3   NAME

_____

Last   First   Middle   Hebrew

GENDER (circle) M F   BIRTH DATE ___/___/___   GRADE ___   E-MAIL ADDRESS_____

MARRIED (circle) N Y   If yes, Spouse's Name _____ Grandchildren's Names _____

ADDRESS (if not living at home) _____

| | Street | City | State | Zip |

ADDITIONAL INFORMATION

Please write any additional information that you feel is important in the space below. Please feel free to use additional pages if necessary.

This membership is valid until _____.

Temple Hesed

1 Knox Road • Scranton, PA 18505

phone: (570) 344-7201 • fax: (570) 344-4514

www.templehesed.org • templehesed@verizon.net

Welcome to Temple Hesed! Please provide the information requested below so we can get to know you and facilitate your involvement in our congregation. (Check box and Specify name /# if more than one adult on the form)

NAME #1 _____   NAME #2 _____

COMMITTEES

STANDING COMMITTEES

☐ Adult Education/Children's Religious Education/Sisterhood   ☐ Book Club

☐ Caring Committee (Visits/Calls to Congregants who are Ill/Homebound/Etc.) ☐ Cemetery

☐ Children's Religious Education (Religious School Programs/Teaching)   ☐ Constitution/By-laws

☐ Finance   ☐ Fundraising   ☐ Investments   ☐ Legal

☐ Membership (Interfaith/College Outreach, Membership Retention)   ☐ *Messenger* (The Newsletter)

☐ Property   ☐ Publicity   ☐ Social Action   ☐ Worship Committee

SPECIFIC TASKS

CHILDREN'S RELIGIOUS EDUCATION

☐ Assist Shabbat/Hebrew School Teacher ☐ Help Coordinate Youth Group Programs

FOOD PREPARATION

☐ Bake for Oneg/Temple Event ☐ Grocery Shop for Temple Event

☐ Prepare Food in Temple Kitchen → → → → ☐ For Temple Events OR ☐ For Member Who Are Infirm

PROGRAMS

☐ Coordinate Adult Education Program ☐ Coordinate Special Program for Religious School

OFFICE SKILLS/TECHNOLOGY

☐ Help with Temple Web-page ☐ Help Design Database for Record-Keeping for Committee/Event Chair

☐ Write E-mails to Go to Membership ☐ Collate Mailing for Special Temple Program ☐ Help with *Messenger*

SHABBAT/HOLIDAY SERVICES

☐ Participate with Honor in Shabbat Service → ☐ Hebrew Prayer ☐ English Only ☐ No Speaking Part

☐ Hesed Welcomer at Shabbat Services ☐ Participate in Musical Service (instrumental or vocal). Specify _____

14   The Outreach and Membership Idea Book Volume III

ARE YOU INTERESTED?

JOIN OTHER GROUPS

☐ _____ (PLEASE SPECIFY)

☐ _____ (PLEASE SPECIFY)

☐ I can't find the right job for my interests, but I want to help. Please call me at _____.

An Invitation to All Jewish Students,
Newcomers to the Community,
and Unaffiliated Jews

Temple Hesed, Scranton's only Reform synagogue would like to invite Jewish students, newcomers to the community, and unaffiliated Jews to join us for High Holy Day Services.

Students and newcomers to the community will be provided with a host family for the holidays, allowing them to share a holiday meal, and to join our Temple Hesed family in prayer and spirituality as we bring in the Jewish New Year.

Contact Temple Hesed at 570-344-7201
for further information and arrangements.

To learn more about Temple Hesed go to www.templehesed.org

TEMPLE HESED
1 KNOX STREET
SCRANTON, PENNSYLVANIA 18505

Date Joined _____   Resignation Date: _____

It is our Temple Hesed policy to conduct an exit interview with each former Temple Hesed member upon his/her resignation. We would appreciate your honest opinion about your membership. You have absolutely nothing to lose by being as frank and candid as possible. Your objective feedback can help us to improve our house of worship. If you wish that your responses remain confidential, please check the appropriate box provided at the end of the questionnaire. Please complete this questionnaire and return it to Marilyn Deutsch. A postage paid self-addressed envelope is enclosed for your convenience. If you would prefer a personal interview please contact Marilyn at mhdeut@epix.net or 570-563-2557. Thank you for your valued opinion.

The main reasons I am leaving (or left) Temple Hesed are: _____

Please circle which best describes your feeling about the following aspects of your Temple Hesed membership. Feel free to be specific with comments.

Worship Services

Very Satisfied   Satisfied   Not Satisfied   Very Dissatisfied

Comments _____

High Holiday Worship Service

Very Satisfied   Satisfied   Not Satisfied   Very Dissatisfied

Comments _____

Rabbi

Very Satisfied   Satisfied   Not Satisfied   Very Dissatisfied

Comments _____

The Temple Board

Very Satisfied   Satisfied   Not Satisfied   Very Dissatisfied

Comments _____

Temple Committees

Very Satisfied   Satisfied   Not Satisfied   Very Dissatisfied

Comments _____

Dues Structure

Very Satisfied   Satisfied   Not Satisfied   Very Dissatisfied

Comments _____

Life Cycle Events   (ex. Births, Bar/Bat Mitzvahs. Weddings, Funerals

Very Satisfied   Satisfied   Not Satisfied   Very Dissatisfied

Comments _____

Friendliness of Congregation

Very Satisfied   Satisfied   Not Satisfied   Very Dissatisfied

Comments _____

Various Activities & Study Groups

Very Satisfied   Satisfied   Not Satisfied   Very Dissatisfied

Comments: (be specific please) _____

Children's Education (Where applicable)

Very Satisfied   Satisfied   Not Satisfied   Very Dissatisfied

Comments _____

Bar & Bat Mitzvah & Confirmation (Where applicable)

Very Satisfied   Satisfied   Not Satisfied   Very Dissatisfied

Comments _____

If you have marked dissatisfied or very dissatisfied on any of the above topics, we would appreciate your additional comments:

Would you recommend Temple Hesed to a friend? Please explain. _____

Is there anything Temple Hesed personnel could have done to prevent you from leaving? Please be specific:

20   The Outreach and Membership Idea Book Volume III

Additional Comments: (please use other side if necessary)

Thank you for your time and effort.

Feel free to share my comments and, if necessary, my name to help improve Temple Hesed.

You may share my general comments but not my name.

Please keep this information confidential to be used for membership purposes only.

Member Name (Please Print) _____ Date: _____

Chapter One   Recruitment   21

SERVICES

Shabbat services are held Friday evenings. Times and dates for special services are published in our bulletin and on our website calendar. We are a very active community with programs that meet the needs of our entire congregation. Several versions of the Reform siddurim are used. Tot Shabbot programs are held monthly, often followed by a covered dish dinner. A monthly bulletin, The Messenger, is a comprehensive publication to keep you up-to-date on all activities and opportunities at Temple Hesed.

MEMBERSHIP BENEFITS

Members in good standing receive: complementary High Holiday tickets; burial privileges for members and their loved ones regardless of faith; Caring Committee services for members in need while infirm, homebound or facing life stress; and opportunities for members of all ages to participate in social action projects as well as social groups.

A WARM WELCOME AWAITS YOU!

To learn more about Temple Hesed, visit our website at www.templehesed.org. We also invite you to visit with us. We guarantee you will find a warm and welcoming environment.

1 Knox Road, Scranton, PA 18505
570.344.7201   www.templehesed.org

Temple Hesed
1 Knox Road
Scranton, PA 18505

Welcome To
Temple Hesed

The Temple of
Loving Kindness

Worship
Education
Social Action
Interfaith Activities
Friendship

WELCOME

Welcome to Temple Hesed, a Union for Reform Judaism member synagogue in Scranton, Pennsylvania. Welcome is a word you will hear quite often in connection with Temple Hesed. We are a welcoming community, open and accepting of all those in search of a spiritual and social home. At Temple Hesed, individuals and families of every age, income and lifestyle will find a warm welcome.

OUR RABBI

We are proud to have Rabbi Daniel J. Swartz as our spiritual leader. Rabbi Swartz brings to our community his warmth, humor, experience and outstanding religious leadership. The Rabbi has a fervent passion for social justice and respect for the environment. An accomplished author and recognized religious and environmental scholar, Rabbi Swartz holds numerous academic honors from Brown University and Hebrew Union College.

"I believe our tradition calls on us to build a world that is not only more just, but also where love for our fellow human beings can blossom."

- Rabbi Daniel Swartz

OUR TEMPLE COMMUNITY

Proudly tracing our history to 1860, Temple Hesed offers a Reform Jewish Program for our approximately 200 member families. Many of our members come from various points from around our nation and around the globe. We have a variety of interfaith initiatives to serve our diverse and growing population. Our programs are flexible to meet the ever-changing needs and practices of our congregation. We strive to serve our members of all ages and family constellations with opportunities for spiritual, educational and social growth. Have an idea for a new program? We would love to hear your thoughts and ideas.

RELIGIOUS EDUCATION

At Temple Hesed, religious education opportunities abound for all.

Hebrew School – Our Hebrew School meets one afternoon per week, typically from 4:30pm – 6pm. The School prepares students from 4th to 6th grade for Bar/Bat Mitzvah.

Shabbat School – Our Shabbat School meets in the spacious classrooms located in the lower level of the Temple. We present a fun and stimulating program to help our children explore the full religious, historical and cultural aspects of Judaism. At Temple Hesed, we also offer an extensive Family Education Program allowing parents to learn with, and from, their children!

ADULT EDUCATION

Temple Hesed offers opportunities for life-long learning. Programs center on not only learning about Judaism, but on how to live more fulfilling Jewish lives.

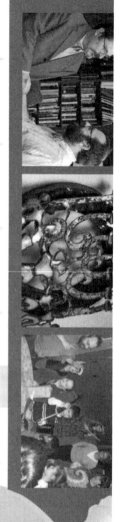

by Michael Weinberg
www.michaelweinberg.com

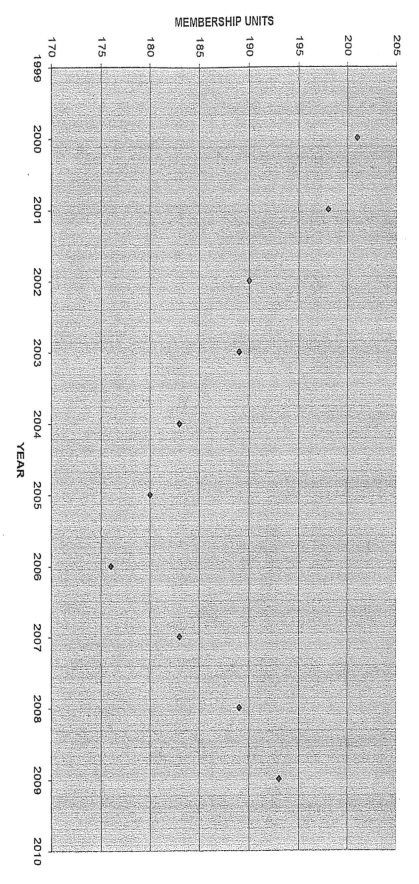

Religious Service Calendar

Baptist

FIRST BAPTIST CHURCH
OF ABINGTON
1216 N. Abington Rd
(corner of Abington & Carbondale)
Come Join Us For
Services Sunday
Morning 11:00 a.m.
Pastor Kenneth Knapp
(570) 587-4492

Catholic

OUR LADY OF THE SNOWS
St. Benedict
SATURDAY VIGIL MASSES
4 p.m. St. Benedict
5 p.m. Our Lady of the Snows
6:30 p.m. Our Lady of the Snows
SUNDAY
7 a.m. Our Lady of the Snows
8 a.m. St. Benedict
9:30 a.m. Our Lady of the Snows
11:00 a.m. St. Benedict
11:15 Our Lady of the Snows
12:20 St. Benedict
CONFESSIONS
SATURDAYS
3:00 p.m. St. Benedict
6:00 p.m. Our Lady of the Snows
(570) 586-1741

Episcopal

THE CHURCH
OF THE EPIPHANY
Church Hill Rd., Glenburn PA
(2 Miles North of Clarks Summit)
Come join us for worship on
SUNDAY
8:00am & 10:30 am
HOLY EUCHARIST
9:00am - Sunday School & Adult
Forum
Nursery Available
WEDNESDAY
9:30AM
HOLY EUCHARIST
563-1564
www.epiphanyglenburn.org
God's heart & hands in the
Abingtons

Jewish

TEMPLE HESED
1 Knox Rd., Scranton
Rabbi Daniel Swartz
http://www.templehesed.org
(570) 344-7201
templehesod@verizon.net
CELEBRATE SHABBAT!
Fridays, 8 p.m.
Accepting Registrations for
Bar/Bat Mitzvah Program
K-10 Sabbath School
Adult Education Classes.
Interfaith Familias Welcome.
Come Join Us!

Lutheran

TRINITY LUTHERAN CHURCH
205 W. Grove Street
Rev. George Mathews Pastor
Worship Services
Saturday 7:00 p.m.
Contemporary Sunday Service 8:15 a.m.
Sunday School 9:15
Sunday 10:30 a.m.
www.TrinityLutheranCS.com
Call our Preschool:
586-5590
Church Office
587-1088

Presbyterian USA

FIRST
PRESBYTERIAN
CHURCH
300 School St.,
Clarks Summit
Worship with us on
Sunday mornings
9:00 & 11:15 am
Church School for
all ages at 10:00
Child Care Available
all morning
Children Welcome!
586-6306
www.fpccs.org

United Methodist

WAVERLY UNITED
METHODIST CHURCH
105 Church Street
Sunday Worship 10:30 a.m.
Nursery Available
Bible Study Sanctuary Handicapped
Accessible
Rev. Barbara Snyder
(570) 586-8166
All Are Welcome!
www.waverlyumc.com
umc.com

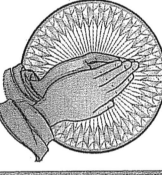

Call 829-7130 To Advertise

Shalom Squad

Congregation:	Congregation Beth Torah
Address:	6100 W. 127th Street, Overland Park, KS 66209
Phone number:	913-498-2212
Contact's Name and E-mail:	Laura Intfen, Lintfen@beth-torah.org
Number of Member Units:	660
URJ District:	Central District
Rabbis:	Rabbi Mark Levin, Rabbi Vered Harris
Membership Chair:	Laura Intfen, Volunteer and Member Service Coordinator

Brief Description: Our Shalom Squad is a group of volunteers trained to welcome and assist everyone who enters our building for Erev Shabbat worship *"panim el panim, yad b'yad"* or "face to face, hand to hand." The Shalom Squad also supports our congregational goal of creating sacred community before, during, and after worship.

Program Goals: Assist in building a sacred community by greeting, offering hospitality, and providing friendly attentiveness before, during, and after worship to all who enter our building.

Target Population: Program targets are congregants and guests attending Erev Shabbat worship.

Number of participants: There are twenty members on the Shalom Squad.

Number and length of sessions: Three volunteers work together for approximately two hours each.

Staffing Required: One staff member to coordinate the volunteer schedule and run training; volunteer congregants.

Total Cost of Program: $150.00 for pins, name tags, and snacks for training sessions.

Source of Funding: Outreach line item.

Logistics: Training session: One handbook per volunteer, refreshments, calendar containing dates for upcoming Erev Shabbat services; Weekly: volunteer shift schedules, pins, name tags.

Instructions to Facilitator: Recruit members of the Squad through face-to-face discussions on Erev Shabbat. Run one training session a year using the attached handbook. Be in contact with volunteers before worship to alert them of any scheduled guests or any congregants needing an overt act of kindness (due to death in family, illness, joyous occasion).

Evaluation of Program: I receive e-mails from both congregants and guests commenting on the warm and welcoming atmosphere that is created by Shalom Squad members. I always ask prospective members how their experience was if I know they attended an Erev Shabbat worship.

Follow-up: At our annual training meeting for new Shalom Squad members, I always invite current members of the Squad to tell success moments and share expertise. I also contact volunteers on the Monday after their shift to check in with them.

Newsletter Article:

If you have attended an Erev Shabbat worship service this summer, you may have noticed something different as soon as you walked in the front doors. We no longer have greeters to welcome you as you come to worship; you are now welcomed by the **Shalom Squad.** This group of volunteers will become even more visible and part of your worship experience when we introduce our monthly Simchat Shabbat celebrations beginning August 19th.

Why the name change? Because these dedicated people are not just there to wish you a *Shabbat Shalom*, but to help create a sacred community within our walls. The Shalom Squad is dedicated to encountering people *"panim el panim, yad b' yad"* or face to face, hand to hand. With the Shalom Squad volunteers in place, guests and congregants are greeted at the front door and welcomed. People who appear lost in the service and unable to find a page in the Siddur can count on someone helping them find their place. Strangers to Beth Torah can feel part of our community as Shalom Squad volunteers strike up a conversation with them during Oneg Shabbat.

You will know a Shalom Squad member by their name tag and bright yellow five pointed-star pin. These volunteers have had training and are educated in the history of Beth Torah, the architecture of the building, and the nuts and bolts of that night's worship. They are aware of the concerns and joys filling the people who fill our building. Ask them any questions you have about Beth Torah when you see them.

Right now our Shalom Squad is coordinated by **John and Alyson Spector**.

The volunteers include: **Travis & Richard Bellotti, Carol Ducak, Mindi Ellis, Amy Franklin, Eileen Garry, Anne Jacobs, Harriet & Ron Jacobson, Marlene Kahn, Vicki Kahn, Robert Kort, Beti Moskowitz, Maureen & Sandy Salz, David Spizman, Heather Swarts Betsy Wanger and Betsy Wilinsky**.

You can help create sacred community here at Beth Torah also. Give me a call at the office and sign up for the Squad, the Shalom Squad that is!

August 14, 2009

Ray Davidson
9046 W. 124th Street #194
Overland Park, KS 66213

Dear Ray,

I am so thrilled that you will be joining the Congregation Beth Torah Shalom Squad. Please find enclosed the Shalom Squad Handbook which contains the job description for this vital volunteer position. It also contains some historical and architectural information about Beth Torah which I think you will find interesting and helpful when starting conversations with visitors.

I will have a name tag and pin for when you come for the training session. Notice these pins have 5 points, corresponding to the five values of the Shalom Squad; which are listed in the handbook.

The Shalom Squad leaders are Betsy Wilinsky (xxx-xxx-xxxx) and Betsy Wanger (xxx-xxx-xxxx). One of these women will be calling you soon to get you on the schedule. Thank you for stepping forward and being counted as you fulfill the mitzvah of welcoming the stranger.

Laura Intfen

Volunteer and Member Services Coordinator
Congregation Beth Torah
(913) 498-2212
lintfen@beth-torah.org

Agenda for Shalom Squad Meeting

- Welcome: Thank you for taking the time to learn how to help create a sacred community.

- Introduce one another and tell your strongest connection to Beth Torah.

- Open to green sheets and do d'var Torah.

- Distribute post-it notes.

- Turn to blue page and read mission statement out loud.

- On the salmon page there are 5 qualities of a greeter. Please review them and take notes on your stickies of the ones that speak to you. Then place the stickies on the wall near the white posters of the Erev Shabbat time schedule where you think your idea will best fit.

- While you are up and writing on the wall, please look at your calendar on the wall. The job of greeter will require at least 2 people on a "usual" Friday night and 6 people on Simchat Shabbat.

- After the activity: As we finish our meeting, it is important to look at the Squad as a sacred community onto itself. On the yellow sheet you will find a roster of the Shalom Squad. On the back of this sheet is a calendar of days.

- Communication with each other is essential. That is why, to assist you with this we are going to set up a Shalom Squad list serve. You can use this forum not only to communicate problems with the system (although you can certainly brainstorm electronically), this would be a great opportunity to increase our welcome. For instance, if a member tells you on a Friday night that his/her mother, brother, child is having surgery/a try out/ leaving on a trip to Israel, put that information on the list serve so the squad members the following week can ask the member how things went. The member walks into a welcoming, warm environment. How wonderful they will feel.

- If you have signed up for a day and can't make it, please call someone on the Squad to fill in. If you can't find someone, please call the new Hospitality chair people: Allyson and John Spector.

- Allyson and John will be training squad volunteers in the future. If someone comes up to you and wants to join the squad please refer them to me or to the Spectors, or take their name and let me know and I will pass the info to John and Allyson.

- On the last page are the connections for what we have learned today and actions we will be taking. As you wear your pin and people ask you about it (and they will), be prepared to explain the Shalom Squad and the 5 core values of a sacred community.

- The goal of this committee now, is to be the initiator of welcome. You are all role models; mentors to the Beth Torah community who will model and exemplify how to be a sacred community. As you show welcome, warmth, and practice *panim el panim, yad b'yad* (face to face and hand to hand), so will others. Communicate with each other, communicate with me, but most importantly, communicate with the people that walk through our door.

D'var Torah for Shalom Squad

Now Adonai was seen by him by the oaks of Mamre

As he was sitting at the entrance of his tent at the heat of the day.

He lifted up his eyes and saw:

Here, three men standing over against him.

When he saw them, he ran to meet them from the entrance to his tent and bowed to the earth

And said: "My lords,

Pray do not pass by your servant!

Pray let a little water be fetched, then wash your feet and recline under the tree;

Let me fetch (you) a bit of bread, that you may refresh your hearts,

Then afterward, you may pass on-

For you have, after all, passed your servant's way!"

They said: "Do thus, as you have spoken."

Abraham hastened into his tent to Sarah and said:

"Make haste! Three measures of the choice flour! Knead it, make bread-cakes!"

Abraham ran to the oxen,

He fetched a young ox, tender and fine, and gave it to a

Serving-lad, that he might hasten to make it ready;

Then he fetched cream and milk and the young ox that he had

Made ready, and placed it before them.

—Genesis 18:1-8

What is the message about hospitality in this text? What words in the text create that message?

Shalom Squad Handbook

Building Sacred Community With Every Encounter

Mission Statement for the Hospitality Committee (Shalom Squad):

Assist the congregation in building a sacred community by addressing the needs of: greeting, hospitality and friendly attentiveness during worship and social opportunities.

Welcome to the Beth Torah Shalom Squad. You have joined Beth Torah congregants dedicated to encountering people *"panim el panim, yad b'yad"* or 'face to face, hand to hand". A welcoming system such as the Shalom Squad can change the whole "feeling tone" of a congregation. Now visitors and guests will not be left to wander in our building, looking for a specific room or person. With the Shalom Squad volunteers in place, guests are greeted at the front door and welcomed. People who appear lost in the service can count on someone helping them find the place. The consistency of striving to reach the goal of sacred community will create a different feel and energy before, during, and after the services. Plus, the Shalom Squad themselves feel good that they have fulfilled the *mitzvah* of *hachnasat orchim*, hospitality."

What are the values on which the Shalom Squad are based?

Synagogue 2000, a national transdenominational institute dedicated to revitalizing and re-energizing synagogue life in North America, teaches the importance of welcoming the stranger in their curriculum, Sacred Community: *Kehillah Kedosha*. Dr Ron Wolfson, co-founder of S2K, emphasizes these points for greeters in synagogues:

1. **Accepting the Other**: The unconditional acceptance of whoever walks into the synagogue is the hallmark of a culture of community. Everyone is made in the image of God. Everyone deserves to be accepted into the community. By offering a handshake and a smile, the gestures say, "You are welcome here." Even if the congregant or visitor responds coldly, it is the task of the greeter "to receive" the person, whatever her/his state of mind is at the time.

2. **Recognizing the Other**: It takes very little effort to say a good word to people as they come into the sanctuary. In addition to the appropriate greeting of the day (*"Shabbat Shalom"*, *"Chag Sameach"*),

add a word or two of a personal nature—"How are the kids?" "How's your Mom doing?" – to recognize the other.

3. **Uplifting the Other**: Sometimes people come to the synagogue in search of encouragement, comfort and peace. Perhaps they have had a frustrating week. They may be coming to say Kaddish for a loved one. Show tenderness and kindness to those who come to shul.

4. **Teaching the Other**: By greeting everyone warmly, you will establish a "climate" of welcome in the group that assembles. Your model of greeting may very well be picked up by others in the group. The modeling is encouraged by our rabbi as he/she invites everyone to "turn and greet" one another as our services starts.

5. **Attending to the Needs of the Other**:

   - **The physically lost**. Be on the lookout for those newcomers and visitors who don't know where anything is in the building. They may be embarrassed to ask where certain things are—the restrooms, the babysitter, and the *kippah/tallit* cabinet. They may be nervous about putting on a *kippah* or *tallit*.

   - **The physically challenged**. People who are disabled may need special help in getting settled in the sanctuary. There is a congregational wheelchair available that is kept in the staff bathroom.

   - **Children**: Be ready to assist children to get comfortable in the service. If a parent looks uncomfortable with their child's behavior, remind them that although children are always welcome in the sanctuary, the parent may get more out of the service and the child may be happier if the parent and child make use of our free babysitting service.

What do I do when it is my turn on the Shalom Squad?

Mark on your calendar when you have signed up. If something comes up and you can not make it, do your best to find a replacement from the roster and let the committee chairs know of the change.

You will receive an email or phone call from the Volunteer and Member Services Coordinator the morning of your assignment. This will let you know the caring and concern items that are important for you to know. Any questions on this communication should be directed back to the Volunteer and Member Services Coordinator at Beth Torah.

Be in place to welcome people ½ hour before things get rolling here. That would mean 6:00 on non-Simchat Shabbat evenings and 5:45 on Simchat Shabbat evenings. You will find your name tags on the Volunteer Coordinator's desk, and you can put them back there at the end of the evening. **Name tags are very important**.

Greet at the front door of the building using the values on which the Shalom Squad is based. At about 6:20 one of the Shalom Squad members can move to the sanctuary door to pass out worship materials. At 6:30, both Shalom Squad members should be at the sanctuary door.

At approximately 6:40, a staff member will shut the sanctuary doors. The Shalom Squad should stay outside the sanctuary doors to welcome people and hand out siddurim. When the trickle of late comers has slowed down, the Shalom Squad members should move inside the sanctuary and position themselves where they can offer late comers open siddurim.

32 The Outreach and Membership Idea Book Volume III

After the services, be positioned by the oneg table to greet people there. Be your wonderful, friendly self!! Strike up a conversation with at least one person you do not know, and introduce that person to someone you do know. This pamphlet contains a FAQ sheet about Beth Torah that has on it great conversation starters.

On Sunday or Monday, please contact the Volunteer and Member Services Coordinator with any caring and/or concern issues that you discovered in your conversations during oneg.

Congratulations!! You have been instrumental in removing barriers of inclusion from the Beth Torah experience!! Thank you so much.

Chapter One   Recruitment   **33**

Quick FAQ sheet on Congregation Beth Torah:

History:

March 27, 1988:	First organizational meeting held in the home of Hal & Carol Sader.
May 6, 1989	First b'nai mitzvah ceremony. Bat mitzvah of Rachel Garron.
January 14, 1990	Approval of purchase of land at congregational meeting.
September 21, 1996	First worship service in the new sanctuary.
November 15, 1996	Official dedication of building.
Rabbi Levin:	with Beth Torah from the start: 1988
Rabbi Harris:	with Beth Torah from June 2000
Jack Feldman:	Executive Director of Beth Torah since November 2006
Marcia Rittmaster:	Director of Youth and Informal Education since 1996
Laura Intfen:	Volunteer and Member Services Coordinator since December 2002
Linda Sweenie:	Music Volunteer since 1997, Music Director since 2004

Some facts about our building:

The architect of the building is Mel Solomon (a member) and the building has won awards for its design.

Stone is used extensively throughout the building. One of the reasons for this references Genesis Chapter 28, where Jacob rests and puts a stone under his head. After his night of dreaming of Jacob's ladder and the angels going up and down the ladder, he names the place where he puts the stone "House of God", as it is where he encounters the divine.

There are seven poles in the oolam. While the structure requires two poles, the architect thought two poles in the middle of the foyer looked awkward. It was a brainstorm to add five more poles. Two of poles are weight bearing and four have lights in them. The one pole that reaches up to the skylight has no work to do. The poles represent the seven days of creation and the tall pole represents Shabbat. A day of no work, of reaching up to God and a day of looking for connecting with all of God's world.

The Heritage Torah: The Heritage Torah was written in 1770 and belonged to Jews in Domazlice, Czechoslovikia. In 1930, the Jewish population of Domazlice was 69. Their synagogue, which was built around 1880, was demolished in 1939.

Torah scrolls and other religious objects were confiscated by the Nazis to be used to establish a museum for a defunct culture once all of the Jews had been annihilated. One thousand five hundred and sixty four Torah scrolls had been stored by the Nazis. Our Heritage Torah is one of those scrolls. Besides its amazing story, it has belonged to two congregations before us. This represents the vein of continuity of a historical community.

Looking out the window in the sanctuary, we see the trees. Trees were prevalent in the first story of Torah (Garden of Eden) and in fact the Torah itself is referred to in the Siddur and rabbinically as the Tree of Life. Leaves are in the pattern of the carpeting found on the sanctuary floor.

There are 36 pews in the sanctuary, 18 on each side. This represents double chai (chai representing life in Hebrew letters).

The wood is of superior quality and a richer color everywhere the Torah touches. This is the top of the amood (reading table), the inside of the ark and the Torah stand on the bimah. This is to remind us of the sanctity of Torah.

The disc on the ceiling of the sanctuary acts as a sound collector, but symbolizes the cloud of God that followed the Jews across the desert. Just as the cloud was there when Torah was received, so was the Kedosh(the light of God) as represented by the skylight in the middle of the disc. There are twelve lights in the front side of the disc representing the Twelve Tribes of Israel. The four lights in the back of the disc represent the four matriarchs (Sarah, Leah, Rebecca and Rachel) and the three lights right in front of the ark represent the three patriarchs (Abraham, Isaac and Jacob). The bimah is elevated to represent Mt Sinai.

The words on the outside of the ark are from Exodus Chapter 3 verse 5 and translate as: "Remove your sandals from your feet, for the place on which you stand is holy ground." The image on the curtain is the burning bush, where the voice of God comes from. The Hebrew letters on the covers of the Torahs in the ark form the Hebrew word for fire (aish).

Weekly Email to Shalom Squad

Thank you for being the CBT Shalom Squad tonight. I will have your name tags on my desk. Here is some k'shrarim (community and caring) items for you to note:

_____ is having minor surgery at 1 today. I don't really know what it is for.

It is _____'s birthday. She is a regular.

_____ son leaves for military training tomorrow in preparation of going to Iraq. She is very worried.

Here are the members observing yahrzeits tonight:

We will be doing service #5 tonight and the music is Shir Balev. There is a Torah Service tonight but no sermon.

Let's hope the rain stops. See you at 6:15. Thank you for all you do.

Laura

Rosh Hashanah under the Stars

Congregation:	Baltimore Hebrew Congregation
Address:	7401 Park Heights Avenue, Baltimore Maryland 21208-5490
Phone number:	410-764-1587
Contact's Name and E-mail:	Joanne Windman, jwindman@bhcong.org
Number of Member Units:	1300
URJ District:	East District
Clergy:	Rabbi Andrew Busch, Rabbi Elissa Sachs-Kohen, Rabbi Paul Sidlofsky, Cantor Robbie Solomon, Cantor Ann Sacks
Membership Chair:	Sally Hendler, Chairperson

Brief Description: We moved our family service for Erev Rosh Hashanah outdoors and invited the entire community to attend for free. We rented a local park that is also used by the Baltimore Symphony. We encouraged people to bring blankets and picnic dinners and to worship with Baltimore Hebrew Congregation.

Program Goals: To remove any stigma associated with synagogue worship; to present an affordable, casual worship opportunity for *anyone* interested in attending; to reach out to the affiliated and unaffiliated, interfaith families, couples, seniors, empty nesters, young families, young adults, and youth; to show another, less formal side of Baltimore Hebrew Congregation.

Target Population: Unaffiliated, interfaith families and couples, young families, young adults, and youth throughout the Maryland area.

Number of participants: 3,500 in 2008.

Number of sessions: In the first year, 2007, approximately 2,500 people attended; in the second year, 2008, approximately 3,500 people attended; and this year, 2009, we expect at least 4,000 to attend. The Rosh Hashanah family service is about one hour in length.

Staffing Required: Rabbi, cantor, adult and youth choirs, two sound engineers, volunteers to set up and clean up, parking lot attendants, security, administrative and maintenance staff

Total Cost of Program: Approximately $35,000.

Source of Funding: Budget and private contributions.

Fee for attendees: Free.

Logistics: Sound system; backdrop for outdoor stage, which was transformed to a bimah and ark; chairs and risers; in 2007 apples and honey sticks were given out after the service; in 2008 seed packets that read "Grow With Us" were given out; tables/chairs for registration. We created a website for preregistration, www.RHunderthestars.com, a separate phone line for an alternate means of registration, lighting, parking lot attendants, security, and a newly created worship service booklet, advertising, posters, postcards, and flyers.

Instruction to facilitator: Secure a public, open location. Create a website registration, worship service booklet, and arrange for an adequate sound system. The clergy worked together on the service and music.

Evaluation of Program: We have run this program for two years now. The community response was so overwhelming we were surprised and now feel obligated to continue. We did not get an overwhelming response to membership. We knew membership gain would be slow, but are thinking long term regarding building an accessible identity for Baltimore Hebrew Congregation, planning that this will play out in membership over the coming years. We did find that the creative worship opportunity filled a need for many people in the community who may be unaffiliated, including interfaith couples and interfaith families. Many attendees actually belong to another congregation but attended Rosh Hashanah under the Stars with other family members who may have been unaffiliated or who were looking for a different worship experience.

Follow-up: We did ask members of our Membership Committee to help with follow-up phone calls and invited everyone to join us for Erev Simchat Torah.

Number 12 August 2007
17 Av – 17 Elul 5767

Rabbi Rex D. Perlmeter
Cantor Judith K. Rowland
Rabbi Elissa M. Sachs-Kohen
Rabbi Emeritus Murray Saltzman

Baltimore Hebrew Congregation Bulletin

Inside . . .

Todah Rabbah	2
From the Clergy	2
New Members	2
Lifetime Achievement Award	3
Community *Shabbat* Dinner	3
High Holy Day Information	4
High Holy Day Schedule	5
Locks of Love Highlights	6
Youth & Young Adult News	7
Hoffberger Gallery	8
Day School Doings	8
PreSchool Prism	8
Religious School *Ruach*	9
Sisterhood in Session	9
Brotherhood News	10
Offerings	11-12
August Events	15
Worship	16

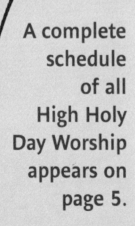

A complete schedule of all High Holy Day Worship appears on page 5.

ROSH HASHANAH
Under the Stars

Wednesday, September 12

Oregon Ridge Park
13555 Beaver Dam Road, Cockeysville, MD 21030

5 PM • Park Opens
6:30 PM • Family Services
Led by Rabbi Sachs-Kohen and Cantor Sacks

All are welcome!

Tickets are required. To receive your FREE tickets log on to www.RHUnderthestars.com or call 443-524-0284.

Special thanks to THE ASSOCIATED for promotional support.

Baltimore Hebrew Congregation
Building Sacred Community.

7401 Park Heights Avenue
Baltimore, MD 21208
410-764-1587 • www.bhcong.org

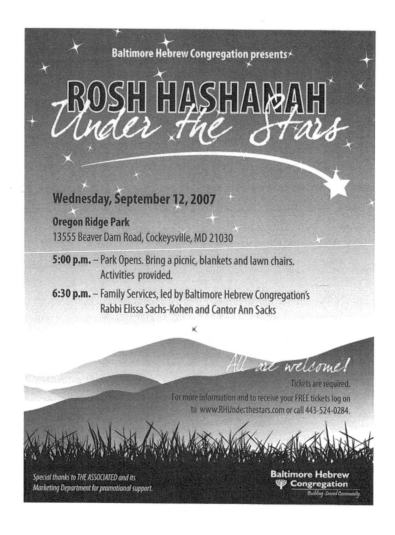
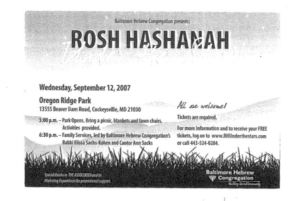

Chapter One   Recruitment   41

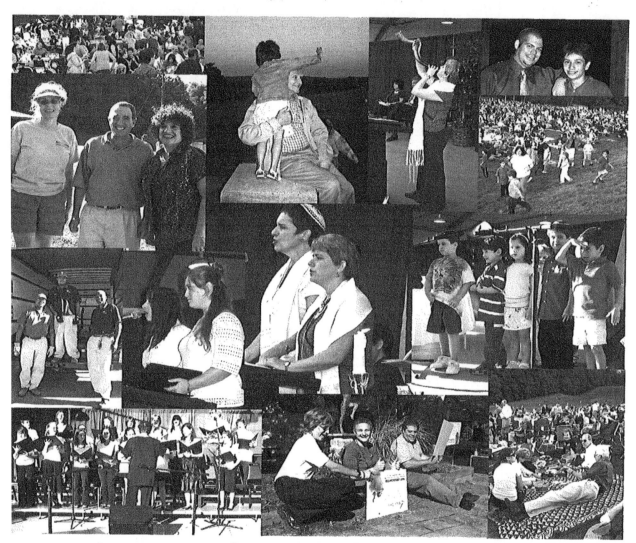

Community Coming Together

Rosh Hashanah Under the Stars" was a memorable life experience for thousands of Baltimore Jews. Kudos to Congregant, Laura lack, for her suggestion to have "*Rosh Hashanah* Under the Stars." This successful worship opportunity was co-chaired by Sally lendler and Dr. Edward Perl, along with a committee of many talented and eager thinkers and workers. Special thanks to Barbara ooper for handling the processing of tickets, to The Associated's Marketing Department and our Congregant Jessica Normington or assisting BHC with a marketing plan, the clergy and staff of BHC who so willingly stepped up to the plate whenever asked, to ndy Wayne, David Berenhaus, Lynda Weinstein and to all of our volunteers who made this event such a success! As a Congregation nd community we are indeed very fortunate. *Kol HaKavod*—Congratulations and thanks to all!

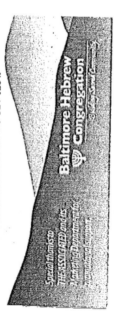

editorial

BHC's Bold Move

Is it cost or interest that's preventing more people from joining area synagogues? The leadership of the Baltimore Hebrew Congregation, with some support from The Associated: Jewish Community Federation of Baltimore, is about to find out.

It's happening with what might be Jewish Baltimore's most expensive outreach campaign yet. (See "Starry, Starry Night," page 28). The Reform congregation is funding, to the tune of more than $1 million, an initiative that includes a free, outdoor Rosh Hashanah concert and service, reduced membership fees in every category, and by making religious school education free to the children of congregants.

BHC expectedly hopes to not only engage inactive members, but gain new ones. If that does not happen, then the 1,325 unit congregation will still have provided valuable lessons for the community at large, helping us all to better understand the realistic capabilities of the Jewish marketplace.

On the one hand, smaller congregations might be jealous. After all, BHC has the major donors to fund this. But it also took vision and risk-taking, something that the Jewish community needs more of and that should be applauded. Not only that, but smaller, similar programs can be tried at other congregations. More important is the philosophy that a rising tide lifts all ships. If more people become interested in Jewish life through this effort, some may join BHC, some may affiliate elsewhere. That's why the Associated is helping out with some marketing guidance, another good use of communal dollars.

Dr. Edward L Perl is pushing the Reform congregation's Membership Enrichment Initiative.

The Catch-22, of course, is that people who are not regularly involved with synagogues cannot understand the positive transformative effects of being active in Jewish life. BHC is out to change that; we look forward to chronicling the results. □

Academic Idiocy

Are universities sanctuaries for robust debate and consideration of all ideas or the crucible of intolerance and bigotry? A majority of members in Great Britain's largest university teachers association, the University and College Union, recently made the latter choice. How else to describe their vote to boycott *all* Israeli universities?

Critics of the move often argue that the Union is targeting Israel while ignoring institutions in China, Syria, Russian, Iran, Sudan and elsewhere. However, to do so lumps Israel with those serial human rights abusers. Israel, like any country, has made mistakes in some policies. However, like any democracy, it openly confronts those problems and allows people to pressure the government through regular elections and parliamentary representation. That can never be repeated enough as the Union simply ignores the dire problems in so many other lands.

In addition, in ending engagement and debate with Israeli scholars and their students, the Union squelches dialogue — including with the many Israeli Arabs at these schools. It also emboldens the understandable distrust of Israel toward Great Britain and its academics.

We stress that not all British scholars agree with the Union's move. In fact, presidents of Britain's leading research universities have declared opposition to the policy and some key British politicians have joined them, according to the Jewish Telegraphic Agency.

How to respond? The New York-based Yeshiva University offers an excellent example. It has asked to be listed with Israeli universities being boycotted. As YU President Richard Joel said on Monday, "This boycott is a threat not only to Israeli academics but also to open societies everywhere."

Not only is he right, but American Jews should follow him in pressing universities across this country to join with pride YU's move. What a statement it would make if world leading institutions such as the Johns Hopkins University, Harvard, Yale, UCLA, Stanford and so many others stopped cooperating with the bigots who now hold sway in England's University and College Union. □

localnews

Starry, Starry Night

BHC to kick off outreach push with free, outdoors Rosh Hashanah service at Oregon Ridge.

Neil Rubin
Editor

In what they hope will become a model for expanding Jewish affiliation here, leaders of Baltimore's largest Reform congregation last week approved an aggressive, $1 million-plus outreach plan.

What's being billed as the Membership Enrichment Initiative begins Sept. 12 with a free outdoor Rosh Hashanah festival and service at Oregon Ridge Park. The Initiative also will include reduced membership fees in all categories, free religious school for member families and enhanced young adult programming. It is being funded by between 20 and 30 congregants, and no costs will be borne by existing membership and program fees, stressed Dr. Edward L. Perl, BHC's first vice president and a key force in the effort.

The congregation, which has about 1,325 membership units, according to executive director Jo Ann Windman, currently has dues that run as high $2,200 — before Hebrew school and other expenses.

"We're doing this because we have seen that in a lot of Reform congregations there has not been a lot of growth, and we don't know if that's from external factors of people not affiliating or something else," Dr. Perl said. "We said let's look at all the factors that could stand in the way of being more attractive and engaging, and let's see what the response is and how we grow."

Dr. Perl said if BHC does not see a bump up in membership and participation — part of the goal being to involve current members who do not frequent BHC programs and services — then the congregation will have learned valuable lessons about its market and capabilities.

The Oregon Ridge event, coordinated by Rabbi Elissa Sachs-Kohen, will begin at 5 p.m. with family activities, picnics and a concert by the Israeli group Seeds of Sun. Then comes the 6:30 p.m. Rosh Hashanah service, followed by receptions for groups such as young adults, families and others. Programming and transportation is being provided for college students.

"We really want to make it open and inviting to everyone, no matter what someone's level or affiliation is — and they won't be getting a letter in the mail asking for money," said Rabbi

PHOTO PROVIDED

Reaching Out: BHC's Dr. Edward L. Perl and others are pushing the Reform congregation's Membership Enrichment Initiative.

Sachs-Kohen, who is developing a prayer book specifically for the event. "We will follow up, but this is not an under-the-cover fund-raiser."

The congregation will still hold its more traditional Rosh Hashanah service for members at its Park Heights Avenue campus.

Those at Oregon Ridge also can receive free tickets to the Sept. 21

High Holy Days head outside

Casual worship part of Jewish outreach

BY LIZ F. KAY
[SUN REPORTER]

As the sun sets tonight, when faithful Jews across the region flock to synagogues to honor creation in services steeped in tradition, thousands of others will gather with picnic dinners in a Baltimore County park.

The event, "Rosh Hashana Under the Stars," will be an informal evening service designed to draw young families and others who might not otherwise celebrate the Jewish New Year.

"When we take it outside, it becomes an event that is much more open and inviting," said Rabbi Elissa Sachs-Kohen, who will lead the service for Baltimore Hebrew Congregation, a Reform synagogue sponsoring the event.

In recent years, congregations around Maryland and across the country have been trying creative methods to reach Jews — particularly young adults — who are unaffiliated with synagogues, whether the barriers are cost or culture.

B'nai Israel Congregation on Lloyd Street is offering a special "beginners" service, as well as free tickets for High Holy Days services to people younger than age 30.

And tomorrow afternoon, Har Sinai Congregation in Owings Mills will hold its fourth annual Tashlich service, inviting people to cast bread crumbs representing their sins into a stream at Meadowood
[Please see HOLIDAYS, 4B]

FROM THE COVER

High Holy Days become outreach

HOLIDAYS [From Page 1B]

Regional Park in Green Spring Valley. Afterward, they'll enjoy a picnic, a shofar-blowing contest and other activities.

Jews who aren't very active in a congregation are more likely to "dip in" for services on Rosh Hashana or Yom Kippur on Sept. 22, said Vanessa Ochs, an associate professor of religious studies at the University of Virginia and author of Inventing Jewish Ritual. The two holidays bookend the High Holy Days, or days of repentance.

Outreach services can attract them. "They're all about being enticing and creating a mood and an environment where someone who might not be likely to come feels welcome," Ochs said.

Participants have been invited to bring a picnic dinner to enjoy before the service begins at 6:30 p.m., featuring contemporary music and creative use of the shofar, or ram's horn.

"We want people to feel comfortable and also challenged and inspired, and we want to reclaim some of the awe and the majesty of worshiping in a beautiful place in the middle of the created world," the rabbi said.

Baltimore Hebrew had to shut down registration early this month after 2,500 people signed up for tickets to attend the hourlong celebration at Oregon Ridge Park in Cockeysville. About two-thirds are not members of Baltimore Hebrew, Sachs-Kohen said.

This service takes the place of Baltimore Hebrew's family service, which about 300 people attended last year.

Although participants weren't asked why they wished to come, Baltimore Hebrew's leaders have heard that some want to bring their kids and not feel as if they're disturbing anybody and that some are interested in the location.

"Others are drawn to the fact that they don't have to wear a suit and tie," the rabbi said.

The free service is part of a "membership enrichment" initiative at Baltimore Hebrew, which includes reduced membership dues and enhanced education programs, said Executive Director Jo Ann Windman.

In addition, the synagogue has eliminated religious school fees, aside from training for bar or bat mitzvah, or confirmation. Overall, congregation members have pledged more than $1 million toward these efforts, including the Rosh Hashana program.

Frank Boches, co-president of B'nai Israel, said about 55 people have signed up for High Holy Day tickets, bringing their estimated total attendance to more than 210. Last year, about 170 people came to services, he said.

The idea grew out of a popular Friday night Shabbat series aimed at young people, Boches said. "We just wanted to keep this going," he said.

The modern Orthodox congregation, on Lloyd Street east of downtown Baltimore, was able to provide tickets thanks to donations from benefactors within the congregation.

B'nai Israel is also holding a shorter "beginner" Rosh Hashana service designed by the National Jewish Outreach Program that will incorporate both English and Hebrew, Boches said. In addition, they have also begun accepting credit cards for payments and will soon allow members to make reservations for holy days online.

"If we have an open heart, we need to have an open door," said Rabbi Alan Yuter. "Sometimes you have to get people in the door to see what you have to offer."

Har Sinai is expecting more than 200 people to come to its Tashlich service, which is aimed at young families. It will be followed by a sing-along, relay races and a bake-off using the traditional ingredients of apples and honey, which represent the sweetness of the new year.

But the event's highlight is the custom of casting breadcrumbs into the stream, said Rabbi Bradd H. Boxman. "The idea is cleansing yourself, freeing yourself to start a new year fresh and clean," he said.

After a traditional morning service, the informal Tashlich is an excellent complement, the rabbi said. "It's not the stuffy kind of service their parents might have gone to," the rabbi said. "That's an alternative to reach people we might not otherwise reach."

liz.kay@baltsun.com

46 The Outreach and Membership Idea Book Volume III

Whatever Happened to the Wandering Jews of Chelmsford?

Congregation:	Congregation Shalom
Address:	87 Richardson Rd., N. Chelmsford, MA 01863
Phone number:	978-251-8091
Contact's Name and E-mail:	Rabbi Shoshana M. Perry, rabbi@congregrationshalom.org
Number of Member Units:	196
URJ District:	East District
Rabbi:	Rabbi Shoshana M. Perry
Membership Chair:	Susan McHugh

Brief Description: At the end of the book of Numbers, in *Parashat Mas'ei,* we are taught that Moses recorded all the various stages of the Israelites' wilderness journey. For example the text begins: "They set out from Ramses in the first month, on the fifteenth of the month. It was on the morrow of the Paschal offering that the Israelites started out defiantly, in plain view of all the Egyptians." The Torah not only records the starting point of each leg of the journey but also periodically offers commentary about the different stages. Why was it important for Moses to meticulously record and remember each encampment? Why was it important after forty years, on the brink of entering the Promised Land, to review these wanderings, stage by stage? The reasons are multifold. First and foremost, those who were about to enter the Promised Land had not even been alive during the time of the enslavement in Egypt, and most of them had probably been born well into the forty-year wilderness experience. Moses understood that this new generation needed to feel a connection to their past, to realize that their parents' history and life experience was their life story as well. Moses also realized that this younger generation needed to own the gift of freedom and to feel a responsibility to carry on the existential story that lies at the heart of Jewish identity. Most of all, Moses understood that for the future to have meaning, the past must be understood and embraced.

Congregation Shalom found itself facing a powerful period of transition. The synagogue was going to be celebrating its fortieth anniversary, and in the prior ten years, the synagogue had doubled in size. Although many of the founding members were still actively involved in the community, the nature of the synagogue's identity seemed poised on the threshold of change. For many reasons (described in the Goals section below) the synagogue decided to make a film called "Whatever Happened to the Wandering Jews of Chelmsford?" We would record stories of our founding members, recall the different stages of our synagogue's growth, and link this journey to our congregation's future. Newer members of Congregation Shalom would have a greater understanding of where we had come from and perhaps gain a clearer sense of our direction for the future. Most of all, we would meet our goals for membership retention and recruitment as well as our commitment to reaching out to the interfaith couples and families of our congregation.

Program Goals: The goals for this program were multifold, but they all fit wonderfully together.

1. We wanted to record the history of our congregation directly from stories told by founding members before their generation was gone. This effort would also be a way to honor some of the most beloved members of the synagogue.

2. We wanted to create a dynamic, captivating venue that would show the vibrancy of Congregation Shalom. We wanted to tell our story in a way that all members, both new and old, would understand. We wanted them to be excited to be a part of the history of Congregation Shalom, to underscore why synagogue affiliation is important. At this level, the DVD was an effort to improve synagogue retention.
3. We wanted to highlight the congregation's commitment from the very beginning to reach out to interfaith families and to restate our desire to be welcoming to all who seek to pursue a Jewish life. The DVD was not to be solely about reaching out to those who were intermarried. Instead we wanted this message to be clear but integrated into the larger picture of who we are. In many ways this goal mirrors the way our synagogue has undertaken all of our Outreach efforts.
4. We wanted to have a professional-quality DVD that would describe what is special and unique about Congregation Shalom and tell our story in a warm, funny, and meaningful way. This DVD would be used in our membership recruitment efforts. We now show it at our New Member Open Houses and we can send it out to prospective members.

Target Population: The DVD is targeted towards all current and prospective members. The DVD also speaks to those who are intermarried and interested in conversion.

Number of Participants: We premiered the DVD at a gala celebrating our fortieth anniversary. There were over 120 people in attendance. We also showed the video to religious school students (grades 3–7). We have shown it at two of our open houses this year and will continue to show it in the future. The DVD is available to our membership committee to send to all interested prospective members.

Staffing Required: The film required a committee of ten people to produce. These people were involved in all stages of its development: production, writing, filming, editing, sound, publicity, etc. All of these people—with the exception of a film editor who was involved in the very final stage of production—were members of the synagogue.

Total Cost of Program: In almost every area the DVD was made by members who donated their time and skills on equipment that was lent to us by a local university. The two exceptions were that we needed to hire a professional film editor to do the final cutting and soundtrack. This cost $750. The costs of copying the DVD were $300. The rabbi covered the expense of the editing through her rabbinic expense line. As the DVDs are sold, the cost of editing is being recouped and the rabbi's budget line is being repaid. The cost of the DVD is $10 and we have sold about fifty copies. The Fund-raising committee donated the monies for copying the DVD, and this donation will go towards helping to cover the use of the DVD by the membership committee.

Source of Funding: Rabbi's budget line, Fund-raising committee.

Logistics:

1. A pre-production committee developed the goals and investigated the options for production, in particular whether to do it in-house or with a professional. If we had pursued working with a professional, the costs would have been upward of $3,000–$5,000.
2. We decided to create the whole film in-house using the talents of our members.
3. We publicized the vision and goals of the film and solicited photos and documents from members. We also developed a list of people to appear in the film, and we invited these members to filming sessions. We included founding members, interfaith couples, converts, and newer and youth members.

4. Each month in our newsletter for over a year we solicited materials, kept the DVD in people's minds with a trivia quiz, and repeatedly advertised the Fortieth Anniversary Gala and showing of the DVD.
5. One of our members was able to borrow professional-quality film equipment from a local university. The sanctuary was set up to be the filming space. Filming was done over several days.
6. Several members took the photo stills that were necessary to make the DVD.
7. Once the oral histories were recorded, one of our members wrote the script. This was then recorded as the voice-over by another member of the committee.
8. We hired a professional film editor (someone our writer/director works with) and together they edited the film and put the soundtrack together.
9. A publicity committee continued to highlight the DVD in our synagogue's weekly updates, newsletters, etc.
10. We had one hundred professional-quality DVDs produced.
11. We premiered the DVD at the Gala. The DVDs were on sale that evening.
12. We showed the DVD in the school after the Gala.

Instructions to Facilitator: When this DVD is used by a membership chair we ask the chair to briefly introduce it and have it on during the time people mingle at the Membership Open Houses. If people would like their own copies, we have them available. Also, if a prospective new member inquires about the history of the congregation and is seeking to better understand the "personality" of the congregation, the membership chair can send a copy of the DVD.

Evaluation of Program: Over time the membership chair will measure the impact through conversation with prospective and new members. He or she will inquire whether the DVD had any impact at all on their interest in affiliation with the congregation. The chair will also inquire which elements of the DVD were most important to people: the oral history, the focus on interfaith families, or the idea that the congregation is a welcoming extended family. We have also informally observed that the DVD was a success with our longer-term members, in that we have sold about fifty copies at a price of $10 a copy to this population.

Follow-up: We will continue to use the DVD in our membership efforts as well as in our efforts to communicate the value of synagogue affiliation. Towards those ends we will periodically show it in our school, and we will suggest that watching the DVD as a family can count towards a child's efforts to become a Bar/Bat Mitzvah. In our congregation students have to do thirteen mitzvot in the categories of study, observance, and deeds of loving-kindness. Watching the DVD could count as one of the study mitzvot.

We also hope to use the DVD in the community. We have several local cable stations in area towns, and we plan on submitting the DVD for use on cable TV. At present we already have two Shabbat services that show once a month on cable TV. We also hope to donate the DVD to local libraries for lending to members of the community.

From the August 2007 & September 2007 Newsletters:

We are working on a documentary in honor of Congregation Shalom's 40th Anniversary and NEED YOUR HELP.

1. We are looking for video footage and/or still photos of Jewish events from the past 40 years.

Footage/photos can be of events held at the temple or of Jewish celebrations in your home.

The types of things we are looking for include, but are not limited to: Bar/BatMitzvahs, any service, holiday party, religious school event, awards presentation, Brotherhood/Sisterhood event, family Seder, etc…

All submissions will be returned in perfect condition.

2. We are also looking for volunteers to help us with this huge project. If you have experience in any aspect of video production and would like to help, please contact us ASAP. We need video camera operators (with own equipment), video editors (own equipment would be helpful) and people experienced with computer generated video graphics.

3. If you have significant stories to share pertaining to important events that helped shape Congregation Shalom, we would like to hear from you. Please email a few paragraphs summing up your story. We're looking for oral histories for possible use in the production.

4. Also, please let us know if you are aware of any "old-timers" who have since moved out of town who can get in touch with us about photos and stories.

Please contact Eileen Hirsch at eileen@shapadv.com or 603-888-2906 if you can help with any of the above.

From the October 2007 Newsletter:

Congregation Shalom's 40th Anniversary Events

Save the Dates! Please join us as we plan the events for our 40th anniversary celebration.

Scheduled events are:

- Middle Eastern Family Event on May 4, 2008
- 40th Gala Event on November 1, 2008

In addition look for Religious School activities and events and further

special announcements as the year unfolds.

50 The Outreach and Membership Idea Book Volume III

From the November 2007 Newsletter:

SAVE THE DATES!

Don't Miss These Exciting Events:

ISRAEL FAMILY FESTIVAL

Sunday, May 4, 2008

Come celebrate our 40th along with Israel's 60th.

Join us for Mid-eastern snacks, Klizmer music and Israeli Dancing.

40th GALA DINNER DANCE

Saturday, November 1, 2008

Reserve the date for an elegant evening of dining, dancing and looking back at 40 years of Congregation Shalom.

ENTER OUR TRIVIA CONTEST!

See how Much You Know About Our Temple.

Every month throughout the year, we will publish, in the newsletter and on the web site, 2-3 Trivia Questions. There are 24 in total. See how many you can answer. The first 2 questions are somewhere in this newsletter! Email your answers to Esther Wikander at emwikander@gmail.com

Plus, look for Religious School activities, additional events and special announcements as the year unfolds!

DO YOU KNOW…

In what year were the Articles of Organization for Congregation Shalom signed? #1

Play the Congregation Shalom 40th Anniversary Trivia Game. Look for 2-3 questions each month in the newsletter and on line. There will be 24 questions in all. Email your answers to Esther Wikander at emwikanker@gmail.com.

Winners will be announced monthly.

DO YOU KNOW…

Why was the name Congregation Shalom chosen? #2

Play the Congregation Shalom 40th Anniversary Trivia Game. Look for 2-3 questions each month in the newsletter and on line. There will be 24 questions in all. Email your answers to Esther Wikander at emwikanker@gmail.com.

Winners will be announced monthly.

From the December 2007 Newsletter:

SAVE THE DATES!

Don't Miss These Exciting Events:

ISRAEL FAMILY FESTIVAL

Sunday, May 4, 2008

Come celebrate our 40th along with Israel's 60th.

Join us for Mid-eastern snacks, Klizmer music and Israeli Dancing.

40th GALA DINNER DANCE

Saturday, November 1, 2008

Reserve the date for an elegant evening of dining,

dancing and looking back at 40 years of Congregation Shalom.

ENTER OUR TRIVIA CONTEST!

See how Much You Know About Our Temple.

Every month throughout the year, we will publish, in the newsletter and on the web site, 2-3 Trivia Questions. There are 24 in total. See how many you can answer. The first 2 questions are somewhere in this newsletter! Email your answers to Esther Wikander at emwikander@gmail.com

Plus, look for Religious School activities, additional events and special announcements as the year unfolds!

DO YOU KNOW...

How much were dues during Congregation Shalom's first year? #3

Congratulations to last month's winner:

Zelman and Ethal Kamein, and Phyllis Kallus.

Answers: #1 – July, 1967. #2 – 6 Day War ended; hope for permanent peace.

Questions #3 and #4 are in this issue.

Send in your answer by Dec. 16th.

Play the Congregation Shalom 40th Anniversary Trivia Game. Look for 2-3 questions each month in the newsletter and on line. There will be 24 questions in all. Email your answers to Esther Wikander at emwikanker@gmail.com.

Winners will be announced monthly.

DO YOU KNOW…

Where and when was the first Congregation Shalom seder held? #4

Congratulations to last month's winner:

Zelman and Ethal Kamein, and Phyllis Kallus.

Answers: #1 – July, 1967. #2 – 6 Day War ended; hope for permanent peace.

Questions #3 and #4 are in this issue.

Send in your answer by Dec. 16th.

Play the Congregation Shalom 40th Anniversary Trivia Game. Look for 2-3 questions each month in the newsletter and on line. There will be 24 questions in all. Email your answers to Esther Wikander at emwikanker@gmail.com.

Winners will be announced monthly.

From the January 2008 Newsletter:

DO YOU KNOW…

Who was the first president of Congregation Shalom? #5

DO YOU KNOW…

From where was torah scroll #1184 rescued? #6

From the February 2008 Newsletter:

DO YOU KNOW…

When did the congregation purchase land on Richardson Rd. #7

DO YOU KNOW…

Who was the first rabbi to be hired? #8

From the March 2008 Newsletter:

DO YOU KNOW…?

How did Congregation Shalom get the ark we currently use? #9

DO YOU KNOW…

When was the first Hebrew School graduation? #10

From the April 2008 Newsletter:

DO YOU KNOW…

In what year was the first classroom wing added? #11

The Congregation Shalom Story:

Whatever Happened to the Wandering Jews Of Chelmsford?

Tape	Time Codes	Subject	BITE/NARRATION
4	23:15 – 23:30	Channah Powell, student	Noah and the animals sailed for 40 days and 40 nights. 40 is like a big number – and it's one of my favorite numbers, actually. I think 40 is really big!"
8	26:04 – – 26:39	Rabbi Perry	"And there's also the time that Moses went up on Mount Sinai to receive the 10 commandments – he was gone for 40 days and 40 nights – and the second time after he destroyed them – he was up there for 40 days and 40 nights. And then our ancestors wandered in the wilderness for 40 years. So I think the number kind of represents largesse. Something big – – Something grand!"
			Cut to title page HAPPY 40th ANNIVERSARY CONGREGATION SHALOM! (use logo?)
8	27:13: – – 27:29	Rabbi Perry	"It's wonderful to see our founding members, to see in their eyes the joy of observing what they've accomplished and built in this community and also it's a great pleasure to see new people coming in and diving in and embracing the congregation as their own."
Montage of talking heads in boxes pop up over a picture of Congregation Shalom			CUE UP MUSIC AND MONTAGE OF SOUNDBITES PRAISING CONGREGATION SHALOM
3	45:57 – 46:04	Ethel K	"We were the first Jewish, formal Jewish institution that ever existed in the Colonial town of Chelmsford."
1	24:41 – 24:47	Roseanne Riddick	"You don't feel like you are performing or competing when you come to Congregation Shalom. You just feel like you belong."
2	29:43 – 29:50	Lynne Rothstein	"Right away you feel like you count here. Right away you feel like you're not just a number. You can play an important role in this congregation – if you want to!"
7	13:33-13:37	Paul Rodman	"Whatever it takes to make something happen, we do it!"
7	29:24 – – 29:26	Danya Degan	"Everyone has a sense of humor around here."
2	15:38—15:44	Chris Michaud	"Congregation Shalom is totally accepting of anyone who comes through these doors."
	18:46 – 18:48		"These people here are special people"
6	2:59 – – 3:06	Rabbi Terry Bard	"It's a community that cares for each other, it's a community that breaks boundaries between people."
8	4:31 – 4:33	Stacy Garnick	"I really feel like it's a place where God lives"
8	34:49 – – 35:00	Rabbi Perry	"Judaism needs to be welcoming. We need to have open doors and invite people in if we are going to continue to thrive as a religion, as a culture, as a people."

Tape	Time Codes	Subject	BITE/NARRATION
Title page			THE CONGREGATION SHALOM STORY: (dissolve in subtitle) WHATEVER HAPPENED TO THE WANDERING JEWS OF CHELMSFORD?
4	02:04 – 02:17	Zelman & Ethel Kamien	"For a while we were called the kissing congregation!" (WHY?) Zelman: "Because we always kissed each other." Ethel: "We all hugged and kissed (laughs) Everybody."
			HOW DO YOU BEGIN TO DESCRIBE A HOUSE OF WORSHIP FILLED WITH SO MUCH WARMTH AND INTIMACY THAT MANY CONSIDER IT A SECOND HOME? HOW DO YOU TELL THE STORY OF A SCRAPPY, DOWN-TO-EARTH CONGREGATION WHERE THE GUY OR GAL READING TORAH MIGHT ALSO BE IN CHARGE OF LANDSCAPING OR THE PLUMBING? AND HOW DO YOU CAPTURE A PLACE WHERE NO ONE REALLY CARES WHERE YOU CAME FROM – IT ONLY MATTERS WHERE YOU WANT TO GO?

Chapter Two

Integration and Retention: Creating Early and Ongoing Connections That Ensure Lifelong Membership

Each congregation enables the creation of a sacred Jewish community. Our congregation's mission should be to create a connection with our new members, integrating them into our community and instilling the value of lifelong membership. How do we create that shared value in our members?

Temple Beth El of Boca Raton draws its members from many different communities. Their **Community Connectors** program brings together groups of neighbors and friends living in the same locale to enjoy social and educational programs. Members interact with clergy, staff, and each other in the intimate setting of a member's home or a public venue within the community. Community Connectors is intergenerational—some gatherings are planned for adults only, and others include families, with programs designed specifically for children. Clergy and staff are there to help the hosts prepare and provide spiritual and educational guidance to all who attend.

Temple Shalom's mission to inspire an enduring relationship with the Jewish people was shown as they gathered friends and newcomers at Shabbat evening services, connecting with them and each other. After Shabbat services, many people had no firm plans for a Shabbat meal or did not know anyone well enough to find a place to go. **Davening and Dining** was created by a dedicated volunteer who gathered together these individuals and families, made reservations to meet at a restaurant after services and created a social opportunity to connect more people to each other, Temple Shalom, and Shabbat.

Congregation Rodeph Shalom's focus on making their synagogue a more welcoming place and an indispensable part of all its members' lives led to their **Open Tent Initiative**. Created to engage the entire congregation, this program asks every congregant to do at least one of five acts—for example, to say hello to a person in the shul they don't know or to bring a nonmember to an event or to services. To remind congregants about their commitment in an effective and memorable way, they created story cards with short personal stories from members about how the Rodeph Shalom community was important to them and how it had impacted their lives.

How do you tell your congregants that they are important to you? How do you find out how they are doing and how the congregation can serve them better? Congregation Beth Am is a large congregation that strives to be a caring and inclusive "house of the people." **Reach Out and Connect-a-thon** was launched as a way to communicate a sense of caring to all of their members by making personal telephone calls to each and every household. Because of these calls, the congregation made sure that every single member had a seder to attend. This effort to connect one-to-one with each member is an invaluable way to meet the needs of every congregant.

Community Connectors Program

Name of Congregation:	Temple Beth El of Boca Raton
Address:	333 SW 4th Avenue
City/State/Zip:	Boca Raton, FL 33432
Phone number:	561/391-8900
Contact's Name and E-mail:	Cara Robbe, crobbe@tbeboca.org
Number of Member Units:	1315
URJ District:	South District
Rabbis:	Daniel Levin, Jessica Spitalnic Brockman,Pamela Mandel
Outreach/Membership Chairperson:	Susan Podolsky
Program Title:	The Community Connectors Program

Brief Description: The Community Connectors Program helps neighbors and friends enjoy social and educational programs right in their own communities, bringing Temple Beth El's sense of family to all. This program allows members to interact with our clergy, staff, and each other in the intimate setting of a member's home, clubhouse, or public venue within the community. Community Connectors is intergenerational—some gatherings are planned for adults only, and others include families, with programs designed specifically for children. Clergy and staff provide spiritual and educational programs that foster Jewish continuity and the goals of the Reform Jewish movement, including the mitzvah of *tikkun olam*.

Events are planned based on the demographics of the members living in the individual community. South Palm Beach County, the direct area from which Temple Beth El draws its membership, comprises many communities that are gated, and this program allows the temple to go "behind the walls" and into the neighborhood. Community Connectors groups are created by virtue of the number of members within a given gated community or zip code. In order to facilitate the connection of member to member, some groups include more than one zip code and more than one community, based on the knowledge of the director of membership or the interests and backgrounds of the members living in those geographic locations.

In communities that are not gated, Community Connectors could be organized by towns or neighborhoods.

The following are examples of typical Community Connectors programs:

- Coffee and Chat or Wine and Cheese Reception with the rabbi
- Sukkah-decorating party
- Chanukah celebration for families, including a mitzvah project for children to help those less fortunate through our *Giving Tree Program*, which distributes holiday gifts to adults and children in need
- Yom Kippur Break Fast
- Passover Potluck

58 The Outreach and Membership Idea Book Volume III

- Break Matzah: end Passover with a pizza party
- Potluck Shabbat dinners
- Purim Hamantaschen baking party
- Havdalah Champagne Get-together

Program Goal: The overall goal of the program is to help members to connect with one another, staff, and clergy, thereby strengthening their connection to our congregation and ensuring their participation as lifelong members. The program also helps to introduce prospective new members to the congregation in a more intimate setting, with the opportunity to meet the clergy face-to-face. The Community Connectors Program helps to

- welcome new members;
- share simchas and sorrows with each other as the spirit of community develops;
- educate and inspire members with innovative programs;
- introduce members within a given geographic location to one another so that lifelong temple affiliation and familiarity can be fostered—"no member shall be left behind";
- provide a vehicle for children to mingle with other children outside of regularly attended Hebrew School and Sunday School classes;
- reach potential new members when those new to our community are introduced to Temple Beth El's mission via the intimate setting of a Community Connectors event.

Target Population: Entire membership plus potential new members.

Number of participants: Presently twenty local communities are organized through the Community Connectors Program, totaling 500 membership units.

Number and length of sessions: Two to three gatherings a year per community. Each program is two to three hours in length.

Staffing required: Each neighborhood has a Community Connector (or several volunteers, depending on the size of the community) who works with the staff at Temple Beth El to

- reserve a date for each event in the rabbis' calendar;
- choose a topic for discussion;
- assist staff in bringing along any materials needed, such as name tags, art supplies, information on upcoming events at the temple, and signage;
- enable the membership and development directors attend whenever possible.

Total cost of program: Staff time is not allocated in the budget; expenses for children's activities, printed invitations, and mailing costs total approximately $700 per year.

Source of funding: Membership budget allocation.

Fee for attendees: Depending on the event, a minimal cover charge may be requested and for some events, members contribute potluck refreshments.

Logistics: Every community engages the help of a Community Connector or group of temple members to serve as the Community Connectors. They engage homes and/or locations outside of the community for specific events. Materials may be added by the clergy or staff for discussion purposes (e.g., photocopies of text). Refreshments are facilitated by the host, Community Connectors, or members of the community. In planning family programs where children are in attendance, our Senior Youth Group, BOFTY, volunteers time to engage children in activities while adults take part in a program pertinent to them.

Instructions to facilitator: The Community Connectors reach out to members of the community with follow-up phone calls and e-mails to encourage attendance, and throughout the year, with messages that extend holiday wishes and notify members about upcoming events that can be shared.

- Exhibit 1: Community Connectors: Recipe for Success (set of guidelines)

- Exhibits 2, 3, and 4: Examples of letters/e-mails sent by Community Connectors introducing the program to members of their community

- Exhibit 5: E-mail card extending holiday wishes sent to members of the community from the Community Connector

- Exhibit 6: Samples of invitations sent in 5768 and 5769

- Exhibit 7: Thank-you letters sent to Community Connector and host by the rabbi following an event

- Exhibit 8: Invitation to Morning of Appreciation from the Membership Committee chairperson to all Community Connectors giving them a chance to meet, mingle, and share ideas

- Exhibit 9: Example of thank-you and holiday wishes extended to Community Connectors by the Membership Committee chairperson

Evaluation of Program: The program began in the fall of 5768 (2007) and the first formal evaluation took place with the clergy, staff, Membership Committee chairperson and Community Connectors in the fall of 5769 (2008). The outcome of the evaluation meeting (Morning of Appreciation) was overwhelming, with lots of positive feedback and sharing of new ideas. Community Connectors walked away with a full understanding that they were valued ambassadors for Temple Beth El, and their help in sharing the mission of our congregation was paramount to the success of our membership retention. Discussion about areas of improvement included the development of better public relations to disseminate information about the program in our monthly *Chronicle*, including photos and brief descriptions of activities. Community Connectors felt that a minimum of two gatherings per year were imperative to accomplish the goals of the program.

Follow-up: The vitality of the Community Connectors Program has reached congregants of all ages and in many communities, resulting in members coming forth on their own to initiate programs in their neighborhoods. With the printing and distribution of our new Membership Directory, *Temple Beth El Community Connector,* a publication that lists the names, addresses, phone numbers, e-mail, and communities of our members, we anticipate that the Community Connector Program will grow by five to ten new communities on a yearly basis. The program has already brought in four new families to our membership, and with expansion into many more areas, we predict that we will acquire more new members in the coming year.

Community Connectors – Recipe for Success

Being a Community Connector is a great way to contribute to our synagogue and help our large synagogue feel smaller and more personal. Your efforts and participation are greatly appreciated. As we continue to take "baby steps" to make this a program that will eventually connect each of our members, we'd like to share the notes from our *Community Connectors Morning of Appreciation* held on September 21, 2008.

Program ideas that have worked:

Holiday Events

Sukkot Family Event

Break the Fast for Yom Kippur

Passover Pot Luck Dinner

Break Matzah Event (At the end of Passover hold a pizza party for all to break Passover)

2nd Night Seder at TBE – Get a table together from the community and celebrate at TBE's seder.

- "Tiki Torah Hanukkah" – have outside and use Tiki Torches as the Menorah
- Have each family bring their own Menorah to light
- Play dreidel
- Hold a "Maccabi" style games – (like an outdoor picnic with sack races, funny relays, etc)
- Tie in a Tzedakah effort to bring a gift for the Giving Tree
- May want to have a children's grab bag for a minimal mount – These are difficult to organize to make sure there are enough gifts for each child that are sex and age appropriate. Books could make great gifts.

Purim – hamantashen baking party. Have everyone come in costume or in masks, or make your own mask party

Events with an Educational and Social Twist

- Evening with Rabbi Dan, Jess or Pam – on topics like spirituality, being Jewish in today's world (Susan has a list from which you may choose or you can create your own).
- Wine and Cheese – "Coffee and Chat"
- Dessert and Coffee – "Coffee and Chat"
  Pool Party

  Family Barbeque

  Shabbat in the homes or clubhouse

  Pot Luck Shabbat Dinner

  Havdalah Event

Process for selecting a date and sending the invitation

Email Susan Podolsky with three possible dates, event location if known and any other logistics.

Susan will coordinate with the rabbi's office to provide any clergy and staff support .

Once a date is selected, you may want to send out a "save the date" to members.

Determine if your community responds best to email invitations or to snail mail and send the invite 6 weeks before the event. If you would like assistance with the invitation, please call Susan.

Follow up with emails to those who have not responded. Phone calls really work well. Try to reach the member rather than leave a message. If you need additional contact numbers, call or email Susan.

Before the event, please send Susan a list so she can forward it on to the rabbi and/or staff that will be attending

Additional notes about planning your event

Think about including a presentation on the West Campus and renovations on the East Campus – NO Solicitation – this is for information only so all members will be informed about the exciting changes we look forward to in 2009 and 2010.

Think about an ice breaker to help people get to know one another especially at the first CC. Susan and Cara have lots of ideas.

The Event

Please plan to welcome your guests and tell them a little about the CC program and why it is so important to you.

After the discussion or activity ask everyone to consider being a host for future CC gatherings, and ideas for new events in the future. Even though no one may come forward in the group, experience has shown that people will do so to you privately.

Take digital photos – it's really such an important touch!

After the event, send an email follow up to thank everyone for coming , thank the host, and announce the next event if you know it. If you took digital photos attach them.

Also send the photos to: sling@tbeboca.org with the event, date and names of people in the photo. Sally tries to put CC photos in the Chronicle's montage. Everyone loves to see their picture and it helps others when promoting Community Connecter events (See, we all had a good time so make the effort to join us!)

Don't do it all yourself – ask for help from others in the neighborhood. Potlucks are great way to get involvement and commitment from others, reduce costs and let people show off with their best dishes! Assign roles to older kids to run an activity for the young kids. Get people to help with the set-up and clean up.

62 The Outreach and Membership Idea Book Volume III

On-going tasks we would appreciate you doing throughout the year

Please create a "group" contact list on your email address book so you can easily send out emails to your community. If you have difficulty creating this contact list, Susan will gladly assist you.

Don't rely completely on email. Many people have spam blockers and your email may not get through their firewall. You may want to call people to make sure they are receiving your email and find out the best way to communicate with members from your community.

Think about finding a partner in your community so you can share the responsibilities and get another member involved.

Periodically Susan will email you and ask you to send an email to your community so that TBE news can easily flow into your communities. This is especially great for the bigger events we share together. (special Shabbats, concerts, dinners, etc.)

Susan will also send periodic holiday wishes that you can "cut and paste" if you'd like and send it on to the members of your community. Holiday wishes include: Rosh Hashanah, Hanukkah and Passover. The group contact list becomes a great tool for this.

When a member of your community becomes a new member of TBE, Susan will email you and ask that you call to welcome him/her/them and explain the CC program to them.

Susan will also send you periodic updates to your master list. Please remember to add the email addresses of new members to your group contacts.

Community Announcements – Community Connectors can play an important role in supporting members for all sorts of activities and life cycle events.

Susan will email you if a TBE member in your community faces a loss. She will include information about the funeral and shivah minyan. Please pass this information to members of your community so everyone can help to organize a minyan and reach out in support and in the spirit of community.

If a member of your community falls ill and/or is the hospital, Susan will also inform you or the member of your community that has become the "Sunshine Committee" so a card and/or call can be made. In the case of a long term illness, it is really nice to organize neighbors to help with meals, carpools, etc.

Susan will email you if a TBE member in your community celebrates a simcha (birth of a baby or grandchild, bar or bat mitzvah, wedding, etc.) Please send an email to the members of your community so everyone can send their congratulations or call with their mazel tov wishes .

Whenever we have a TBE event that has table seating, it is always a great idea to send an email asking members of your community to create a table together.

As your community's Community Connector, you are an important ambassador for Temple Beth El as you continue to communicate the mission of our congregation.

On behalf of the Membership Committee of Temple Beth El, we thank you for your efforts and for your support of this vital program.

Dear Temple Beth El Neighbor,

As fellow members of Temple Beth El of Boca Raton and living in the Boynton Beach area we have a special *connection* in our devotion to our Temple.

Temple Beth El would like to build on this common *connection* with our special *Community Connectors Program*.

Consider these possibilities:

1. We could enjoy many of the benefits of Temple Beth El together either at the Temple or potentially here in our own community with neighbors and new and old friends.

2. Periodically we could have a Shabbat dinner at one of our homes or elsewhere, and then join together for services.

3. We could plan a group activity in our vicinity and invite one of the members of our clergy to join us for an engaging and inspiring discussion.

4. If we want to enable our friends and neighbors who are not Temple Beth El members to learn about our congregation's spirit and warmth and to get to know each other, we could create that opportunity right in our very own community.

5. We could develop a support system for each other for simchas and in times of need.

6. Most importantly, we will be able to experience the warmth, vitality and friendliness of the caring community we have at Temple Beth El as we get to know one another.

The possibilities for connection are endless.

This letter is being sent to all Temple Beth El members in zip codes 33437 and 33436 with the hope that our *community connection* in Boynton Beach will thrive and grow.

Please call us at 561-736-5110 after you read this letter and share your thoughts for planning our first activity.

We'd love to get the ball rolling this summer! We want your involvement, and we look forward to hearing from you soon.

Sincerely,

Gail and Irwin Cohen

Dear Temple Beth El Friend,

Temple Beth El would like to help its members feel a stronger connection to the Temple using an outreach program within the local communities called, "The Community Connectors." I have volunteered to help organize it within Woodfield Hunt Club I and II.

The idea is to "connect" with our neighbors who belong to Temple Beth El. There are currently 23 families living in WHC that are also Temple members and we feel "Community Connectors" can be helpful in informing our community of upcoming Temple events, welcoming new members, spreading the word about families commemorating life cycle events, as well as arranging carpools.

Additionally, we would like to plan an event this year for members in the community. The following ideas have been suggested:

- Shabbat dinner or oneg Shabbat with the rabbi who will lead an informal discussion

- Pot Luck dinner

- Sunday Brunch-get to know your neighbors

- BBQ or pool party

- Dessert under the Sukkah

- Hanukkah Party with latkes

- Purim Party with hamentashen

- Israeli meal-celebration of the 60th anniversary of Israel

- Coffee and Chat or Wine and Cheese study session with the rabbi

Please let me know if you are interested in participating in our community group and which of the above suggestions appeals to you the most. Of course if you do not wish to receive any emails, I will remove you from the list.

Very truly yours,

Trish Schaum

July 22, 2008

19 Tammuz 5768

Mrs. Tracey Grossman
19163 Two River Lane
Boca Raton, FL 33498

Dear Tracey:

Thanks so very, very much for putting together the Community Connector event hosted by Jill and Mitch Ludwig last week. I had a wonderful time spending the evening with members of the congregation I know well, and those I am just beginning to know. I deeply appreciate all your thoughtful hard work that went into making the evening such a success.

This is only the beginning. With the leadership, creativity, and outreach from you as a Community Connector, Temple Beth El can foster the warmth and intimacy that makes our community so special. I hope that we can spend more evenings together, and spend time building our friendship.

Thanks again.

L'Shalom,

Daniel Levin
Rabbi

Hello,

Even though you don't yet know me, we already have a lot in common! We belong to Temple Beth El and live in Saturnia. There are a whole bunch of us, yet we do not all know one another. Wouldn't it be great if we did? That way we could carpool to Hebrew school or services or have someone to attend TBE events with.

This fall Temple Beth El is instituting a new program called Community Connectors. This program aims to foster a sense of community among TBE members who live near one another. My name is Tracey Grossman and Karen Benrubi and I are the Saturnia liaisons.

Our goal this year is to help you connect to TBE in many different ways, one of which is to enjoy activities and programs with friends and neighbors. Additionally, we will help spread the word about families commemorating life cycle events. We want to enjoy programming together and to support one another through good times and bad.

Karen and I will be organizing a Saturnia event later this fall, either a wine and cheese or a barbeque, so that we can meet each other and begin to put names to faces. If you have any ideas or want to help plan that, please let me know. **However, since we want to get to know you before then**, we hope that you will attend **Blue Jeans Shabbat** on August 24th. Dinner is at 6pm at TBE and we would love to put together a Saturnia table for that event.

Please do me a favor, email me back and let me know that you have received this note and if it is okay to include your email address on mass emails to the Saturnia community. And, let me know if you are planning to attend Blue Jeans Shabbat, have school aged children and would like to carpool with other Saturnia members.

Thank you for your time. We look forward to meeting you!!

Tracey and Karen

Other Upcoming Temple events are:

- Information re: High Holidays and tickets will be mailed end of July

- **Blue Jeans Shabbat**-August 24th-6pm dinner and 8pm service. Welcome Rabbi Pam Mailender and reconnect with friends-$10.00 per person. RSVP to 391-8900 ext. 213

- **Girls Pottery Night Out** with WRJ-July 25th at 7pm: A "crafty" evening with snacks and fun. To reserve send $25 to TBE and mark envelope WRJ Pottery Nite

- WRJ **Book Review and Dessert Potluck**-Tuesday, August 28th at 7:30pm RSVP to Jill Cross at 338-3572

- **TBE Film Festival** August 15th at 7:00 at TBE, free showing with dessert reception – Sponsored by Brotherhood

Chapter Two   Integration and Retention   **67**

Exhibit 6

Meet and Mingle with Old and New Friends and Neighbors.
Make this your Temple Beth El Connection!
Please join us for lunch in Beth's newly renovated home.

You're invited
to our first
"33432" -TBE

COMMUNITY
**CONNECTORS
LUNCHEON**

"Creating a Jewish Home"

Join our Rabbis, Cantorial Soloists
and Susan Knight, Interior Designer

WHEN: MARCH 26TH 11:30-1:30 LUNCH

WHERE: 234 ALEXANDER PALM ROAD
ROYAL PALM YACHT AND COUNTRY CLUB

RSVP TO: BETH ZIPPER 393-6060
JBZIPPER@BELLSOUTH.NET

NO SOLICITATION - JUST RELAX AND ENJOY!!!

Camino Lakes   *Carriage Hill*   *Palm Beach Farms*   *Boca Square*   *Boca East Estates*   *Boca South*   *Marina Del Mar*   *Camino Gardens*

Please join us on

Sunday, March 30 4:30 – 6:00 pm

At the Home of

Nancy & Gary Eisenberg

67 SW 12 Terrace, Boca Raton

For a Wine & Cheese Potluck to "Meet & Greet"

Your neighbors within our Beth El Community!

It is important to RSVP to nsefla@aol.com or 561.368.3572

Bring your favorite Wine or Beverage or Cheese and Crackers to Share!

(This is an adults only event, but family friendly fun is being planned for the future)

Sponsored by "Community Connectors", a subdivision of the Membership committee of Beth El, providing opportunities throughout the year for members to meet and mingle with other members in their neighborhoods

Palmetto Park Terrace   *Spanish River Gardens*   *Royal Oak Hills*

"No Solicitation"

Chapter Two Integration and Retention

Please join

The Eastside Connection

Sunday, October 19th

4:00 – 6:00 pm

at the home of

Jill & Michael Cross
541 SW 15th St
Boca Raton

for a Sukkot Celebration

Please RSVP to jillyc1217@aol.com or (561) 338-9976

by October 15th

Come help decorate the Sukkah

and then we'll enjoy a Potluck Dinner together.

Sponsored by the Membership Committee's "Community Connectors" Program
We provide opportunities to help Temple Beth El members "get connected".
Please come to meet new friends and mingle with old friends as we build community together with
Boca East Estates ~ Boca South ~ Boca Square ~ Camino Gardens ~ Camino Lakes ~ Carriage Hill
Palm Beach Farms ~ Palmetto Park Terrace ~ Royal Oak Hills ~ Spanish River Gardens
Your Community Connectors
Nancy Eisenberg ~ Amy Lagala ~ Anna Pincus ~ Susan Sosin

A Morning of Appreciation
planned especially for our Community Connectors

Please Join Me

for Bagels and Coffee

Sunday, September 21st
9:30 am
In the Frances & Solon Cohen Atrium at Temple Beth El

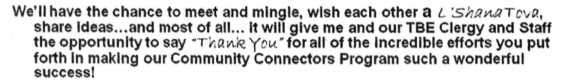

We'll have the chance to meet and mingle, wish each other a *L'Shana Tova*, share ideas...and most of all... it will give me and our TBE Clergy and Staff the opportunity to say *"Thank You"* for all of the incredible efforts you put forth in making our Community Connectors Program such a wonderful success!

Please RSVP to Susan Podolsky at skp714@aol.com by September 15th
I can't wait to see you!

Susan Podolsky

Exhibit 9

The Story of the Maccabees still speaks to us today

Wishing you light that inspires you and all the blessings of a beautiful Hanukkah shared with family & friends

With gratitude to you for all that you do for our Community Connector Program Happy Hanukkah with love,

Susan   5769

Davening and Dining

Name of Congregation:	Temple Shalom
Address:	6930 Alpha Rd., Dallas, Texas, 75252
Phone number:	972-661-1810
Contact's E-mail	Rabbi Andrew Paley, apaley@templeshalomdallas.org
Number of Member Units:	846
URJ District:	South District
Rabbis:	Andrew M. Paley, Jeremy S. Schneider
Outreach/Membership Chairperson:	Meredith Marmurek

Brief Description: Dinner and Davening was created by a dedicated volunteer who gathered together individuals and families who were attending services regularly. It quickly became apparent that many people either had no firm plans for a Shabbat meal after services or did not know anyone well enough to find a place to go. The volunteer coordinated a place to eat after services, maintained a database of current and past participants and attended services weekly to connect more people to each other. In addition, a weekly e-mail was sent out announcing the restaurant location after services and an announcement was made at services each week.

Program Goal: In connection with Temple Shalom's mission to inspire in our congregation an enduring relationship with the Jewish people, the programmatic goal is to gather with friends and newcomers to Temple Shalom at Shabbat evening services, to connect with them and each other, and to increase Temple Shalom's commitment to being a warm and welcoming community.

Target Population: The target populations are Temple Shalom members and all who attend Shabbat evening services.

Number of Participants: The number of participants ranges from twenty-five to sixty. RSVP is preferred but not required.

Number and Length of Sessions: The program is ongoing and occurs each Friday night.

Staffing Required: Staffing is done entirely by volunteers.

Total Cost of Program: There is no cost to the program.

Source of Funding: None is needed.

Fee for Attendees: The fee for attendees is the cost of dinner at the restaurant.

Logistics: The logistics for maintaining the program are in the e-mail that is sent to past participants. The e-mail list is maintained by the volunteer and an announcement about the dinner is made at Friday-night services for dinner immediately following services. Arrangements are made with a restaurant informing them of our arrival time and approximate number of guests.

Instructions to Facilitator: The instructions to the facilitator are to choose a restaurant, gather some friends, and enjoy good conversation and connections!

Evaluation of Program: The evaluation of the program is simple: Outstanding! A huge success! It is easy to maintain and easy to continue. This is the best example of the kind of community for which we strive.

Follow-up: This is the second year of the program and it is still going strong. We do not feel the need to end this program or change its current structure. The volunteer follows up with each new person and new names are forwarded to the congregation's membership secretary.

Announcement placed in weekly email reminders:

Davening and Dining

Each week, this group enjoys comraderie, conversation and cuisine at a local restuarnt. Join us and "C" for yourself how much fun it is to meet new people and enjoy a meal together! Dinner times vary depending on the time of Shabbat or holiday services. This group is open to everyone! To receive the weekly email with dining details and RSVP information, please email Toba Reefer, the group's organizer. Thank you Toba!

Sample Bima announcements:

1. Tonight's Davening and Dining will meet at **Rockfish**, located at the Northwest corner of Coit and Campbell. Davening and Dining welcomes everyone. Join us for great conversation, camaraderie and cuisine immediately following tonight's service.
2. Tonight's Davening and Dining will meet at **Venezia Italian Café**, Audelia Road south of Spring Valley in Richardson. Davening and Dining welcomes everyone. Join us for great conversation, camaraderie and cuisine immediately following tonight's service.
3. Tonight's Davening and Dining will meet at **India Palace** on the southwest corner of Preston and LBJ. Davening and Dining welcomes everyone. Join us for great conversation, camaraderie and cuisine immediately following tonight's service.

Sample Emails sent to participants:

This is a reminder that we are eating at a new Italian Restaurant~Venezia Italian Café~908 Audelia Road, Suite 500, Richardson, TX 75081~972-889-8559. You are encouraged to BYOB to Venezia!

Included printed directions….

Estimated Time: 9 minutes Estimated Distance: 4.58 miles

I am out of town this Friday.
Jerry and Lonna Rae will be your hosts this week.
Please rsvp to Jerry at jerrysil@tx.rr.com and let him know if you can make it on Friday the 27th.

Take care and see you in March, Toba

Open Tent Initiative

Congregation:	Congregation Rodeph Shalom
Address:	615 North Broad Street, Philadelphia, PA
Phone number:	215-627-6747
Contact's Name and E-mail:	Catherine Fischer, cfischer@rodephshalom.org
Number of Member Units:	988
URJ District:	East District
Rabbis:	Rabbi William Kuhn, Rabbi Jill Maderer, Rabbi Michael Holzman
Membership Chair:	Michael Hauptman

Brief Description: The Open Tent Initiative is a consciousness-raising campaign to engage the entire congregation in an effort to make Rodeph Shalom a more welcoming place, as well as an indispensable part of all our members' lives. This program asks every member of the congregation to do at least one of the following five acts:

- Welcome a Stranger: Say hello to someone at the synagogue that you may not know.
- Give a Name: Tell someone on the Membership Committee about someone who may want to join the synagogue.
- Spread the Word: Post upcoming synagogue events at your office or gym to create a buzz.
- Host a Dinner: Invite a new member to Shabbat dinner at your house.
- Bring a Friend: Bring a nonmember to an event or to services.

The challenge was finding a way to remind congregants about this program in an effective and memorable way.

What resulted was a "story-card" campaign that included short personal stories from congregants that described a time when being part of the Rodeph Shalom community was important to them and might have changed their lives. Each card included a reminder to do one of the five welcoming acts. The cards were distributed at services, left on tables around the building, published in the Bulletin and included in packages sent to prospective members. More and more congregants submitted stories.

Program Goals: To make the congregation a more welcoming place for new and prospective members; to encourage stronger connections between members; and to increase the number of visitors. This program was designed to raise the consciousness of the entire congregation about welcoming and what Ron Wolfson calls "radical hospitality" and to reinforce the synagogue's position as a sacred community.

Target Population: The entire congregation.

Staffing Required: Volunteer-led.

Total Cost of Program: Printing costs: $300–500.

Source of Funding: Synagogue budget.

Logistics: Someone must be in charge of the program; we had a three-person committee that collected stories, edited them, designed the cards, and had them printed. Having a graphic designer on the committee was a real benefit!

Instructions to Facilitator: The story cards, while very effective, are just the vehicle for bringing the program to the congregation. It is important that the clergy be totally on board with the program and to make *welcoming* a strong message from the bimah. Articles in the newsletter, posters in the hallways should all emphasize the same message: *everyone is responsible for one act of welcoming.* Each synagogue that initiates this program may have its own unique, customized way of getting the message across to its congregants.

Evaluation of Program: Although evaluation is based mostly on observation and anecdotal evidence, there is no doubt that Rodeph Shalom has had enormous success in getting the message across to enough of the congregation to make a difference. Strangers are now greeted, events are better attended, congregants host brunches and dinners, and people bring nonmembers to more and more events. New and prospective members have commented on the sea change in warmth and welcoming that they have felt in the year since the program was implemented. They say that their first year of membership was filled with invitations, warmth, and inclusion—comments previously unheard at Rodeph Shalom.

Follow-up: We continue to monitor the program to keep it fresh. After publishing twenty story cards, it may be time to find another vehicle for keeping the five welcoming acts on everyone's agenda. The Open Tent Committee will be exploring other ideas in the coming weeks.

Open Tent Initiative:

Welcome the Stranger
Next time you see someone at RS that you don't know, *introduce yourself.*
It could be the start of a beautiful friendship.

Spread the Word
You can help create a buzz about RS.
Post a notice about an event at your office or gym.

Bring a Friend
Think about bringing a friend to RS for a service or an event.
We're always ready for company.

Host a Dinner
Invite a new member to your home for dinner.
Nothing builds community like good food and conversation.

Give a Name
Know someone who may be interested in RS?
Give their name to the Membership Committee, and we'll do the rest.

...just a few samples...

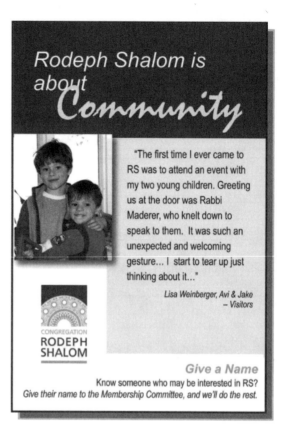

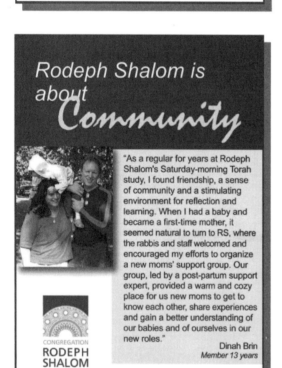

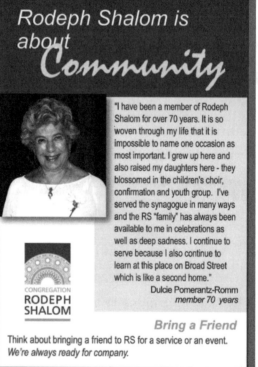

Chapter Two   Integration and Retention   79

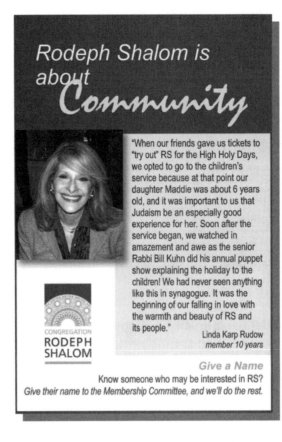

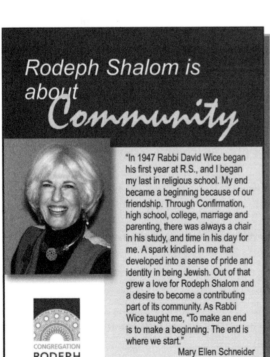

Reach Out and Connect-a-thon

Congregation:	Congregation Beth Am
Address:	26790 Arastradero Road, Los Altos Hills, CA 94022
Phone number:	650-493-4661
Contact's Name and E-mail:	Debbie Coutant, Executive Director, debbie_coutant@betham.org
Number of Member Units:	1485
URJ District:	Western
Rabbis:	Rabbi Janet Marder, Rabbi Josh Zweiback, Rabbi Sarah Wolf, Rabbi Adam Allenberg, Rabbi Jennifer Claymon
Membership Chairs:	Joanne Donsky, Marlene Levenson

Brief Description: Congregation Beth Am is the spiritual home to 1,500 member households. We strive to be a caring and inclusive "house of the people." The Reach Out and Connect-a-thon was launched as a way to communicate a sense of caring to all of our members by making personal telephone calls to each and every household. Chaired by a volunteer, Dawn Crew, and assisted by members of the Membership/Community Committee, including committee cochairs Joanne Donsky and Marlene Levenson, and two of Beth Am's Program Team members, Rabbis Adam Allenberg and Josh Zweiback, more than one hundred volunteers were recruited for two-hour shifts on a Sunday afternoon in February. Instructed to bring their cell phones, they were given a training session, calling scripts, and reply cards to complete following each call.

The Connect-a-thon supported our effort to make sure that everyone in the congregation had a seder to attend. Callers asked if members were interested in attending a seder at another member's home or, if they were hosting one, whether they could accommodate additional guests.

Program Goals:

- To let everyone in the congregation know that they are important and cared about.

- To find out if congregants were interested in attending a Passover seder at another member's home or, if they were hosting one, whether they could accommodate additional guests.

- To obtain updated family data to complete the congregational database.

- To provide an opportunity to discover whether or not a particular congregant might benefit from a direct and confidential referral to one of the rabbis.

- To remind each household to please attend the upcoming annual meeting, at which a very important resolution would be proposed.

Target Population: The entire congregation.

Number of Participants: 110 volunteer congregants; clergy and educators; administrative support.

Chapter Two   Integration and Retention   **81**

Number and Length of Session(s): One Sunday afternoon session from 2 P.M. until 8 P.M., with six one- to two-hour shifts.

Staffing Required: Rabbi Adam Allenberg, program director, and some administrative staff.

Total cost of program: $200 for supplies. Food was donated by volunteers.

Source of funding: Membership/Community Committee budget.

Fee for attendees: Free.

Logistics:

Materials needed:

- Heavy stock paper (A form for each household was designed and printed on heavy paper. Volunteers used these forms to record information gathered. The forms were then directed to clergy, staff, and Seder Matching volunteers for follow-up.)
- Labels: Each form had a label attached with contact information—name, address, phone, and e-mail—for a congregant household.
- Pencils and miscellaneous office supplies
- Cups, napkins, plates
- Printed materials for volunteers, including script
- Large plastic containers for sorting completed forms
- Long extension cords for volunteers to charge their cell phones
- Beverages (purchased)
- Other refreshments (provided by volunteers)

Room Setup: One large meeting room and three smaller classrooms were used. Tables and chairs were set up for the callers. Extension cords and power strips were placed near each table to accommodate cell-phone chargers. One smaller room was set up for volunteer check-in, and pick-up and drop-off of caller forms. Another room was set up for orientation/training. And one more room, next to the callers, was set up with refreshments.

Childcare: None provided

Instructions to facilitator: Organize an event committee, including staff or clergy liaison, to

Clarify goals for event

- Our goals were specific to upcoming programs that would be most successful with personal invitation.
- This program also gave us an avenue to obtain information that was lacking from our database that was easier to gather from a person directly as opposed to a typical mailing with low response.

Book appropriate spaces and clear the calendar with all important parties

Recruit volunteer callers

- This was a massive effort because of the number of volunteers needed to successfully pull off 1,500 phone calls in one afternoon. This required a great deal of support from each and every member of the Program Team (clergy, educators, and administrators)

Publicize the event

- We made sure not to publicize too early in the year, but once we were six weeks before the event, we made sure that everything in every publication and communication included information about the Connect-a-thon. There were two phases of our publicity:

  - Phase 1: Recruiting volunteers. We made sure to publicize through all normal avenues but every member of the staff, the Membership/Community Committee and the Connect-a-thon Organizing Committee made time to personally solicit individuals to be volunteers and callers.

  - Phase 2: Letting the synagogue-at-large know that we would be calling on a given day between certain hours to have a short, personal conversation with them.

Develop materials and forms needed

- This includes publicity materials, signs for the Connect-a-thon, sign-up forms for volunteers (though we did use a hybrid model, using an online form as well as a hard copy), orientation/training materials, and caller scripts.

- We went through a number of drafts of each of the above, but none more than the post-call reply card to record information gathered during the phone call. This way we could guarantee that each caller would record the correct information in a uniform way.

Organize event—check-in, training, food, collection of forms, cleanup

- It is important not to overlook the amount of labor that goes into these steps. For the principal facilitators to take all of this on would drain their collective energies before the Connect-a-thon had even begun.

Follow up

- This required several steps:

  - Each card had to be filed into different categories: follow-up, confidential, seder-matching (host/guest)

  - Any reply card marked for follow-up by more than one person required copies of that card be made and routed to the appropriate people.

- One lesson learned: The Program Team, especially clergy, had not blocked enough time in their schedules to follow-up immediately following the Connect-a-thon. There is a short window of time when a follow-up phone call is still appropriate and effective. Waiting too long can be counterproductive.

Evaluate

- Two to three weeks after the event, the Core Working Group got together to discuss and evaluate the goals accomplished, unforeseen goals accomplished, challenges that emerged and ways to improve the program for the coming year.

Chapter Two   Integration and Retention   **83**

Evaluation of Program: All goals of the program were achieved.

- All 1,500 households were contacted. About half were reached in person. Messages were left if there was no answer. All homes were called at least once. Many (including those where a person was not reached) were phoned multiple times.

- The Connect-a-thon was an excellent public relations effort, greatly appreciated by the recipients of the calls.

- More than thirty-five member households were matched with seder host families. These members would not have had a home seder to attend without this program. Host families reported that they took pleasure in sharing the holiday with new friends.

- The congregational database was updated, providing important membership information for clergy and administrative staff.

Follow-up:

- Seder-matching

- Updating database

- Clergy, educator, and executive director follow-up of requests for calls by congregants

Lessons Learned: First, there are several things that we plan to change for this year's Connect-a-thon (March 15, 2009): We have many Russian-speaking families within our congregation who speak only Russian. This year we will sort those Russian speakers out beforehand and make sure that they are called by another Russian-speaking member. The space, too, was very important. Ours was far too large and carried an echo. Several smaller spaces would have made it easier for our callers to converse freely without interruption or being disturbed by other callers. It is important to have an orientation session running at all times (every twenty minutes) as our callers rarely arrived before their shift was to begin and we found it wasteful to have them wait for the next training. Our calling logs should have recorded the names of the callers (in case follow-up was needed). Callers should not promise a "call-back" as there was no system in place to continue these calls. The member records that were distributed failed to indicate current or past involvement in various areas of synagogue life (*e.g.*, past presidents were mixed in with everyone).

Second, there were many positive surprises in people's reactions to the campaign: Our publicity for this event as well as the beginning of each phone call reminded folks that this call was not a solicitation for funds but an inquiry into people's lives. The weather took a turn in the hours leading up to the Connect-a-thon and we had people in the parking lot greeting our volunteers and carrying umbrellas for them—everyone greatly appreciated this! As we expected, there were several people who shared pastoral needs with the callers that we were able to refer to the clergy. There was an incredible energy in the room amongst the callers and amongst those called. This event really did inspire a sense of connection between our members.

Lastly, we want to address lessons that affect the overall work of the Membership and Community Committee: The biggest impact of the Connect-a-thon on our work was starting a conversation and suggesting a new model for ways to communicate with our members and connect those members to each other. The synagogue board of directors has spent a great deal of energy discussing how we can truly foster a sense of belonging and connection for and between our members. We believe strongly that this event played a role in pushing that conversation forward. A strong relationship and coordination between the professional team and our lay team meant that the day felt organized and successful. Everyone seemed to enjoy themselves and the partnership we created. Having a strong and charismatic lead organizer of the Connect-a-thon also seemed to influence the ease with which all of the details came together. Her enthusiasm for the task at hand and a clear vision of the day's events were essential to our success.

Looking forward, we are now able to see challenges that lie ahead in trying to repeat our success from last year. We are already feeling that doing this every year consecutively might dampen the enthusiasm for the event. We are now thinking about organizing this every other or every third year.

Congregation Beth Am Connect-a-thon Caller Script

Overview for Callers:

An overarching goal of the "Reach Out & Connect" is to communicate a sense of caring community to all Beth Am members. There are three specific purposes.

1. To ensure that we identify the members of our community that would like to attend a Passover Seder and members who can accommodate additional guests.

2. To gain a common set of information about our members.

3. To invite members to the Annual Congregational Meeting.

Caller Guide:

"Hi, _____, this is _____ calling from the Beth Am Connect-a-thon Campaign team. Before I begin, let me assure you that this is not a fundraising call. Can you take 5 minutes to talk now?

(If not, ask when you can call back today and record on the Caller Form.)

Thanks for making the time for us. It's really important to us to be able to connect with all of our members.

As you may know from reading the Beth Am Builder and Menschlink , today is the "Reach Out and Connect–a-thon." We are phoning each Beth Am member household to connect with them for a few reasons.

First, we want to talk about Passover to make sure that everyone who wants can participate in a Seder. We have a number of members who have offered to celebrate the holiday with other Beth Am members. Do you have plans or would you like to be connected with a local Seder?

> **For those having their own Seders:** It is a mitzvah to welcome strangers at your seder. Might you have room at your Seder table for additional guests? (If yes,) Great, how many can you invite? **(Note information on the Caller Form.)** The Seder-matching team will be in touch with you in early April.

> **For those wanting a Seder:** Let me gather the details on your family and preferences so I can pass your information on to the team that will try to match you with a local Seder. **(Note information on Caller Form.)** They will be in touch with you in early April.

Second, we want to ensure that our member records are as complete as possible. One thing we would like to know is:

> **Do you have parents or adult children living in the area? (Please note on Caller Form.)**

Finally, we want invite you to the Annual Beth Am Congregational Meeting. We hope that you can join us on Sunday, April 27 at 4:00. There will be important things to discuss and vote upon. Would you please be sure to save the date, Sunday, April 27 at 4:00 p.m.

That's it from my side. **Is there anything that I can do for you** at this point?

(Listen, take notes on Caller Form.

If there is a highly sensitive topic, please gently transition the conversation and ask if this information can be shared with the appropriate person. Let the person know that what they are saying will be confidential.)

Thank you again for your time and, (if relevant) thank you for your willingness to host. I look forward to seeing you at Beth Am. All the best. Good bye.

Script for a phone message:

Hi, this is _____ from Congregation Beth Am. I'm calling to check in as part of our Reach Out and Connect-a-thon. We hope all is well with you.

If you are interested in hosting a few of our members for Passover, or if you would like to be invited to a Seder, please go to the Beth Am website, www.betham.org and click on the notice about signing up to be a host or a guest at a Seder. Or, you can call Lori Shaffer at 650/494-7008.

Also, we want to invite you to Beth Am's Annual Congregational Meeting on Sunday, April 27 at 4:00. There will be important things to discuss and vote upon. Please save the date: Sunday, April 27 at 4:00.

We are sorry we missed you. Thanks for your time.

Affix label here:

Please check the appropriate follow-up:

☐ **Seder:** ☐ ☐host ☐☐ attend
☐ Clergy
☐ Permission to refer?
☐ Other:_____

Congregation Beth Am Reach Out and Connect-a-thon
February 24th, 2008 | 18th Adar 1, 5768| Caller Form
Caller Form

Called at: _____   Call Back at: _____   Message left_____

_____

Passover Seder Match

☐ ☐Host   How many can you accommodate? _____

☐ ☐Attend

Ages of family members: _____ _____ _____ _____ _____ _____

Details and/or expressed preferences:

Do you have parents or adult children living in the area?

Parents:

Adult children:

Additional notes and comments:

Beth Am Connect-a-thon
Frequently Asked Questions (FAQ)

What is the Beth Am Connect-a-thon?

The Beth Am Connect-a-thon is a one day event where approximately 150 members of our community will come together and call the other 1350 members of our community. It could be compared to a mini "Super Sunday" effort – **without the fundraising!**

Why are we having this event?

We are holding this exciting event in order to:

- to communicate a sense of caring community,
- to make sure everyone has a Seder to attend (and to find members who will provide room at their Seder)
- to learn about family members who may not be in our database

When is it?

The Connect-a-thon will be held on Sunday, February 24th from 2:00-8:00 PM

Where is the event taking place?

The event itself will take place on the Beth Am campus in the Bet Kehillah and surrounding classrooms.

How can I help?

There are three primary ways that you can help. They are:

1. Recruit callers to come to the event on 2/24 and make connect calls
2. Come to the event on 2/24 and make connect calls
3. Provide onsite assistance on 2/24

What do I do to register to help?

There are three ways you can register to help. They are:
1. Complete a registration form (see the end of this document) and send it to Congregation Beth Am, 26790 Arastradero Road, Los Altos Hills, CA 94022, Attention: Dawn Crew
2. Register online (much easier!) at http://www.betham.org/connectathon.html
3. Send an email to the event chair Dawn Crew at dawn_crew@yahoo.com

What should I bring if I am signed up as a caller?

You should bring your cell phone and charger. Each caller will make calls using their cell phone.

What if I do not have a cell phone?

Please let the event chair, Dawn Crew, know when you register. Her email is dawn_crew@yahoo.com. We will have access to a few additional phones.

How will I know what to say when I call people?

We are working hard on a caller guide for each and every caller. When you arrive for your shift, we will have a short 15 minute review and mini training for all of our callers.

How long will I be calling people?

We are asking each caller to come for a 2 hour shift. That will be approximately 1 ½ hours of calling in total. We would like each call to last approximately 5 minutes. Remember, this is a simple and quick connection to our members. We want the experience to be pleasant.

How many calls will I make?

Each caller will start with 15 member call logs. We hope that each caller can connect with at least 10 members during their shift.

What if I do not connect (i.e. nobody answers)?

We ask that you leave as short message and then return the cards to the appropriate onsite person when you leave. If possible we will make additional attempts later in the day to connect with those members we did not reach.

Will there be food?

Will there be food?! This is Beth AM; of course there will be food! Phyllis Karel is already envisioning the best spread to motivate and nourish or callers.

Will it be fun?

This is supposed to be a fun event. The laughter, energy and spirit that we all bring to this community event will certainly add a dimension of fun and enjoyment to this important work.

Will there be childcare?

We will provide supervision for kids ages k-5th grade. Please let the event chair know when you register so we can accommodate everyone.

Beth Am's "Reach Out and Connect-a-thon"

A phone campaign so you know we care!

Registration Form

Beth Am's Membership/Community Committee is kicking off a great effort to let you know we care! On Sunday, February 24, hundreds of Beth Am community members will come together in the Beit Kehillah and make phone calls to each and every one of our members, including you! Join the fun of making these calls.

The purposes of this campaign are to actively communicate a sense of caring community to all our members, to make sure that everyone in our community has a Seder to attend, and to gain a common set of information about our members that will help us continue to communicate with and care for each other.

Come and join in a day of community-building!

Yes! I am happy to volunteer for one of the time slots below.

Please check off the time slot(s) below:

2:00 to 4:00 _____ 3:00 to 5:00

4:00 to 6:00 _____ 5:00 to 7:00

6:00 to 8:00 _____ 7:00 to 8:00

This length of time/the times do not work for me.

I can volunteer from _____ to _____.

I would like to _____ make calls and/or _____ do other things to support callers, like help with welcoming callers, refreshments, distribute/collect information sheets, etc.).

Sorry, I can't help this time.

Name(s): _____

email address(es)(please print): _____

Telephone: _____ Cell: _____

You can also sign up on the web at http://www.betham.org/connectathon.html or send your form to Congregation Beth Am, 26790 Arastradero Road, Los Altos Hills, CA 94022, Attention: Membership/Community Committee

For more information, contact Dawn Crew at dawn_crew@yahoo.com.

Publicity for Connect-a-thon

Information for Beth Am's weekly email update, the Menschlink.

This ran for three weeks.

Join the fun of community-building at Beth Am's Connect-a-thon! On February 24, hundreds of Beth Am members will get together to call every Beth Am household. Please register online <add link> for a short shift as a caller or supporter of this very special event. If you have any questions or would like additional information, please contact Dawn Crew at 650-280-6759 or connectathon@betham.org

See also attached articles from the monthly Beth Am Builder.

PRESIDENT'S MESSAGE

STAY CONNECTED

When my phone rings with a call from a charitable institution, sometimes I find myself gritting my teeth. Not that I don't want to give, but I find it hard to maintain a generous spirit. On Sunday, February 24, every member of Beth Am is going to get a phone call from us, but *we won't be asking for money!* Instead, we'll ask how things are going, and how we at Beth Am can do a better job of connecting with you. As part of our Caring Community-building, we're holding a "Connect-a-Thon" to reach out to every member in a six-hour span on a Sunday afternoon.

In these short calls, we want to "check-in" with Beth Am members: How can we make our community work better for you? What things are you most interested in? We also want to make sure everyone has a place to go for Seder: Can we help find you an invitation? If you are holding a Seder, can you host a few others?

Calling 1,500 people is no small task, and we need 150 volunteers to help us (each will serve a two-hour shift). It's going to be a hectic, fun afternoon, and this is an easy way to get more involved. We guarantee you'll have a great time, be well nourished, and make some new connections. Please call the office, or send an email to Joanne Donsky: *Donsky@sbcglobal.net* or Dawn Crew: *dawn_crew@yahoo.com* to sign up for a shift, and convert a dreary February afternoon into added strength for our very special community.

So when your phone rings on that Sunday afternoon and someone says, "Hi, I'm calling from Beth Am," please take advantage of this opportunity to help find one thing that will make Beth Am more special to you, your family, and all of us.

I'd love to hear your feedback—I can always be reached at *president@betham.org*

SHABBAT SERVICE SPEAKER
ZACK BODNER, AIPAC REGIONAL DIRECTOR

FRIDAY, February 8, 6:15 p.m., Beit Kehillah

Zack Bodner has spoken to groups throughout this region on everything from the U.S.-Israel relationship, to Israel-related policy on Capitol Hill, to the geo-political climate of the modern Middle East, to the importance of grassroots political involvement. As AIPAC's Pacific Northwest Regional Director, Bodner works with Jewish communities in Northern California, Washington, Oregon, Northern Nevada and Alaska, organizing the political and grassroots efforts of pro-Israel activists. His portfolio includes congressional briefings, lobbying, grassroots organizing, political party work and coalition building.

The American Israel Public Affairs Committee is the only American organization whose sole mission is to support Israel. For nearly 50 years, AIPAC has worked to strengthen the relationship between the U.S. and Israel by lobbying Congress about legislation that strengthens the partnership between the two democracies. Headquartered in Washington, the organization has regional offices throughout the country. The Pacific Northwest Region, can be reached at *sf_office@aipac.org* or (415) 989-9140. Visit AIPAC on the web at *www.aipac.org*

CONGREGATION BETH AM
(650) 493-4661
26790 Arastradero Road
Los Altos Hills, CA 94022

JANET R. MARDER Senior Rabbi	rabbi_marder@betham.org
JOSH D. ZWEIBACK Rabbi	rabbi_zweiback@betham.org
DEBBIE COUTANT Executive Director	dcoutant@betham.org
ADAM ALLENBERG Rabbi/Program Director	rabbi_allenberg@betham.org
LAUREN R. BANDMAN Cantor	cantor_bandman@betham.org
INNA BENJAMINSON Émigré Program Director	inna_emigre@betham.org
MICAH J. CITRIN Rabbi	rabbi_citrin@betham.org
MANDY EISNER Director of Development	meisner@betham.org
SARAH LAUING Youth Advisor	slauing@betham.org
ELLEN LEFKOWITZ Educator (Hebrew Program & Shabbaton)	elefkowitz@betham.org
SHERRIE ROSE MALESON Gan Ami Director	srmaleson@betham.org
ROBYN SIEGEL Educator (Sunday Program)	rsiegel@betham.org
SHAINA WASSERMAN Educator	swasserman@betham.org

RABBI SIDNEY AKSELRAD (z"l)
RABBI RICHARD A. BLOCK
CANTOR DAVID UNTERMAN
CANTOR KAY GREENWALD
Emeriti Clergy

BOARD OF DIRECTORS

CHARLES ROTHSCHILD	President
DAN SIEGEL & BEN LLOYD	Vice Presidents
MARK HOLTZMAN	Treasurer
ANDY ROBIN	Secretary
RACHEL TASCH	Member at Large
AMY ASIN	Past President

ANN DEHOVITZ, JOANNE DONSKY,
JEFF HICKMAN, BORIS KELMAN,
KAREN KRONICK, MARILY LERNER,
MARK OSTRAU, REBECCA RUBINSTEIN,
LOUISE STIRPE-GILL, TIM TAICH,
NEIL TUCH, LAURA YECIES

AUXILIARY PRESIDENTS

SAM SHAFFER	Beth Am Temple Youth
JOANN KUKULUS	Beth Am Women
AMIR MATITYAHU	Beth Am Men

THE BETH AM BUILDER

MERRY SELK Editor	builder@betham.org (510) 524-1733
SUSAN WEEKS Design	builder@betham.org (510) 858-1033

We invite members to submit stories and event notices for upcoming issues of the *Builder*. So that issues will reach members' homes on a more timely basis, the final deadline for each issue is five weeks before the issue date—i.e., the 22nd of February is the final deadline for items for the April 2008 issue. Early submissions are greatly appreciated.

Chapter Three

Outreach: Helping All to Find Their Place in Jewish Life

The mission of Outreach, to welcome the stranger, is a core value of Reform Judaism. We encourage all who are interested to join us in the joy of living a Jewish life. This invitation to consider Jewish choices can be extended in many ways—here we explore several of them.

Baderech is a program developed by Temple Emanu-El that provides a carefully matched mentor to each prospective convert, offering encouragement and guidance through the mentoring relationship. The mentor helps the prospective convert make connections and participate in the Temple Emanu-El community. By the end of the conversion process, the new Jew has been closely integrated into the community.

Here in North America, we sometimes forget how incredibly diverse the Jewish world is. As our open tent continues to welcome people with many ethnic and racial backgrounds, we need to sensitize our congregants about the great diversity of our community. Leo Baeck Temple has a number of families that combine Jewish and Asian backgrounds, either through intermarriage, conversion, or adoption. **Celebrating Our Diversity** uses the Chinese New Year to broaden their community's cultural awareness. Leo Baeck Temple families join together in celebrating the overlapping histories of two magnificent traditions, as well as the richness and diversity that reside within the words "Jewish identity." This program can be adapted to celebrate the diverse populations in your congregation.

Many students who participate in basic Judaism classes are newcomers to Judaism, or are seeking an opportunity to deepen their knowledge and appreciation of Jewish concepts, worship, and practice. Some of these individuals may be considering or working toward conversion or they may be in an interfaith relationship and wish to be married by our clergy. When the class ends, where to go? What to do? Congregation Beth Israel's **Integrating Basic Judaism Students into the Life of the Synagogue** is designed to integrate these students into their congregation and ensure their continued involvement long after the course is over.

Jewish children of interfaith marriages are now old enough to share their experiences about growing up in an interfaith family. We can learn so much from them! Ohef Sholom Temple's panel discussion composed of teenage **Jewish Children of Interfaith Families** showed those who attended that vibrant Jewish life can take place in interfaith homes. The response to the panel was so strong that four new interfaith programs were developed to fill the needs expressed by members.

Baderech (*On the Path*)

Name of Congregation:	Temple Emanu-El
Address:	8500 Hillcrest Rd., Dallas, TX 75225
Phone number:	214-706-0000
Contact's E-mail:	Diane Einstein, deinstein@tedallas.org
Number of Member Units:	2600
URJ District:	South District
Clergy:	Rabbi David Stern, Rabbi Debra Robbins, Rabbi Oren Hayon, Rabbi Asher Knight, Cantor Richard Cohn
Outreach Chairpersons:	Amy Seals, Vice Chair: Jane Larkin

Brief Description: *Baderech* is a program that provides a carefully matched mentor to each prospective convert, and through the mentoring relationship, offers encouragement, guidance, and connections as the prospective convert participates in the Temple Emanu-El community. The mentors attend a ninety-minute training session to learn about the conversion process at Temple Emanu-El and their conversion requirements for the coming year. They are also given *Baderech (On the Path)—A Guide for Mentors* (see attached), which provides additional guidance and resources. Both prospective converts and mentors fill out a questionnaire (included in Guide) to facilitate making an appropriate match. In addition, a brief phone interview (outline included in Guide) is conducted with each conversion student. Once these are complete, the cochairs meet with the Choosing Judaism teachers and the associate program director, and students are matched with their mentors.

Program Goal: This one-year (minimum) program is a path of learning, engagement, and friendship, with the mentor's goal being to help the prospective convert find a spiritual home at Temple Emanu-El.

Target Population: Conversion students and mentors who are active members of Temple Emanu-El

Number of participants: This is based on the number of conversion students in a given class, but we train more than enough mentors so that each student is paired up with the right match.

Number and Length of Sessions: We will provide the ninety-minute training session twice a year. Mentors only need to attend the training session once.

Staffing Required: One staff person.

Total Cost of Program: The cost is for printing and copying of materials, and purchasing binders and dividers for the Guide. We also provide snacks and drinks for the mentor training session.

Source of Funding: The Outreach budget.

Fee for Attendees: Free.

Logistics: For the training session we set up round tables that seat eight people. We provide the mentors in attendance with a listing of the Guide contents, a mentor training outline, and a "common situations" guide. We wait until the end of the training program to provide them with the Guide. We supply food and drinks. We also had a dry erase board to display the agenda for the meeting and write down any questions.

Instructions to Facilitator: The *Baderech* Mentor Training Session (see attached) was facilitated by the cochairs of the *Baderech* program. After a brief welcome and explanation of their personal commitment to the conversion program, Rabbi Knight led the group in a text study about the story of Ruth. Next, several active temple members who had completed the conversion process were invited to tell their personal stories to the group. Using an outline and some brief notes, facilitators then gave an overview of the program, including expectations, goals, and suggested activities for mentors to do with their students (included in Guide). A brief question and answer session followed.

The facilitators then led an interactive discussion by describing several of the most common situations that conversion students face or questions they might ask their mentors (included in Guide). After a brief discussion, the facilitators gave the mentors specific advice and strategies for handling these situations and questions with their students. The facilitators then explained the steps that would follow now that training was complete and matched each mentor with a conversion student.

The facilitators also distributed the *Baderech (On the Path): A Guide for Mentors*. The contents of the Guide were explained, and the session concluded with assurances that the cochairs were ready to help the mentors in any way needed.

Evaluation of Program: We received excellent feedback from the mentors who attended the training session. Some of them had previously been mentors, and others had been asked for the first time, but both old and new found the training helpful and were thankful to know exactly what was expected of them. They also greatly appreciated the Guide, which included specific resources they could use as they served as mentors.

Follow-up: Our *Baderech* cochairs will follow up with both the students and the mentors three months after they have been assigned to ensure that they have been matched with the right person. Because we see the mentor as the person who is primarily responsible for the relationship, the cochairs will follow up at six-months and nine-months to ensure that the prospective convert will be integrated into the Temple Emanu-El community.

Baderech Program Mentor Training Session

The training session lasts approximately 1½ hours.

Welcome and Introductions: *Baderech* co-chairs Amy Seals and Penny Coney

Text study: The Story of Ruth, Rabbi Asher Knight

The Conversion Journey at Temple Emanu-El (explanations of each):

- Stepping Stones
- Choosing Judaism
- Working with rabbi
- Mikvah and ceremony

Voices of Jews by Choice:

Several Jews by Choice have been invited to speak for approximately 5 minutes on their conversion experience and to explain how their *mentor* helped them as they went through the conversion journey.

Baderech Program Overview:

Why it is needed to help converts make transition.

Your role as mentors

- Why you were chosen (Temple involvement, good match with CJ student based on interests, children, age etc.)
- Suggested activities to do with your student
- Expectations: how long you'll be mentor, how often to meet, etc.
- Questions about the program?

Common Situations—Interactive Discussion (see attachment):

- How do I know if I'm ready to convert?
- Making the "Announcement"
- Funny, you don't…
- Will I always be called a convert? What will other Jews think?
- Someone asked me, "Why would you want to be Jewish?"
- Oy to the World: The December Dilemma
- Lessons Learned by a Convert Who Has Been There: Some Responses for Mentors

Chapter Three　Outreach　**97**

Nuts and Bolts:

- The Handbook for Mentors
- You've Been "Matched"
- Making the first contact with your Choosing Judaism Student
- What if it isn't a good match?
- Getting help—resources/people to call

January 2009

Dear *Baderech* Partners,

Thank you in advance for the sacred journey you are about to begin with the men and women who are choosing to live their lives as Jews in our community. We are grateful to have you as partners, with them and with us their clergy teachers, along this path of learning and celebration.

Our most important stories from the Torah are about being baderech, on the path, on the road, from one place to another place, making our way from the mundane to the holy. We make our way, *baderech,* with Adam and Eve from Eden out into a world that needs our help to make it whole. We make our way, *baderech*, with Abraham and Sarah, from Haran to Canaan to affirm our faith. We make our way, *baderech*, from Egypt to Sinai with Moses and Miriam, as we become a community of covenant and commitment. We make our way, *baderech*, as a diverse community, to the promised land of Israel to build a home founded on freedom and responsibility, with creativity and hope and spirit.

The *Baderech* Program at Temple Emanu-El is a way for conversion students and members of our congregation to walk together on these same paths toward a dynamic and meaningful Jewish life. Your commitment to walk with our students along these paths toward holiness is a blessing for them and for us. Thank you for sharing your time and your spirit, thank you for opening your heart and your home, thank you for being willing to walk, *baderech*, on the way with us.

B'virkat Shalom,

Rabbi Debra Robbins

Chapter Three   Outreach   **99**

Baderech Guide Contents

Welcome
- *Baderech* Mission Statement
- Temple Emanu-El Core Values
- Temple Emanu-El Outreach Committee Mission Statement

Baderech Mentors
- *Baderech*: The Mentor's Commitment
- The Mentoring Year
- Mentor Profile
- Choosing Judaism Student-Mentor Relationship Matching Questionnaire
- *Baderech* CJ Student Phone Interview Questionnaire
- Guidelines for the Mentor: Welcoming Your CJ Student and Initiating the Mentoring Relationship
- Outreach Becoming a Jew: Questions & Answers (from the URJ website)
- What do I do if…?

Conversion Journey at Temple Emanu-El
- Conversion at Temple Emanu-El
- Questions for *Gerut* (Conversion), Temple Emanu-El

Torah & Reflections
- The Converts
- A Sinai Sea of Jews By Choice
- From Chametz to Rosh Hashanah
- Thoughts on Conversion: Advice From Converts, To Converts
- Head Count
- Jews By Birth Are Also Jews By Choice
- Living a Jewish Life, Living in the Jewish Community, Self-Identifying as a Jew
  - How Do I Know When I'm Ready?
  - A Personal Statement from Mike Willey
  - My Journey into Judaism by Frank Giardina
  - Personal Statement from Penny Coney
  - Always, There is a Mountain … by Amy Seals

Resources

Outreach Readings

- Rabbi Schindler's Address, Dec. 2, 1978

- Excerpt from Rabbi Yoffie's Address at the Houston Biennial, Nov. 19, 2005

- Recommended Reading: Outreach and Membership Bibliography, from URJ website Outreach section

- Outreach Contacts

Baderech Mission Statement

Baderech – "on the way/path" – is a program which provides a mentor to the prospective convert, and through the mentoring relationship, offers encouragement, guidance, and connections as the prospective convert participates in the Temple Emanu-El community. This 1-year (minimum) program is a path of learning, engagement, and friendship, with the goal of helping the prospective convert find his/her spiritual home at Temple Emanu-El.

Temple Emanu-El Core Values

Temple Emanu-El is a vibrant Reform Jewish community that strives to be a place of sacred encounter. It is a place where learning, prayer and deeds change people's understanding of themselves, of their world and their responsibilities in it.

We affirm the power of Jewish learning to create and deepen Jewish identity and commitment. Life-long Jewish learning—from childhood through adulthood—brings Jewish values to our daily lives, nurtures spiritual experiences, and both anchors and challenges us to reach out to a world in need.

We celebrate the potential of prayer to help us reach out to God, root ourselves in community, and affirm the most deeply held values of our people and our faith. Jewish observance at home and at Temple nurtures and inspires both faith and deed. We see the creation of enriching Jewish homes as a fundamental obligation of synagogue life.

At Temple Emanu-El, the creation of a vibrant and meaningful community is both an enduring value and an ongoing endeavor. For us, community means a sense of warm welcome, meaningful relationships, and mutual responsibility. We affirm a sense of both valued boundaries and a great respect for diversity. We celebrate our identity as a multi-generational community. We envision the relationship between congregants, clergy and staff as a partnership based upon mutual respect, shared Jewish commitment, and ongoing Jewish growth. That relationship is manifested in a governance structure that is democratic and reflects the diversity of our congregation.

We emphasize the ethical ideals of social justice at the core of the Jewish tradition. This covenantal obligation frames our actions in terms of our relationship to God and to Jewish tradition. It is Temple Emanu-El's obligation to engage in the ongoing task of world repair. We value being an integral part of and contributor to the total Dallas community.

As Reform Jews, we exist in vital relationship to our own movement and to the Jewish people as a whole. We understand that a fundamental connection exists between Temple Emanu-El and the Jews in Israel and the rest of the world, and we acknowledge our responsibility in promoting the concept of pluralism in the Jewish world.

Temple Emanu-El
Outreach Committee Mission Statement

***May this synagogue be, for all who enter,
the doorway to a richer and more meaningful life.***

Temple Emanu-El actively welcomes interfaith couples, families and individuals seeking to become closer to the Jewish people. Our Outreach Committee creates opportunities for the exploration of Judaism. We support individuals and families who are seeking to strengthen their connection to Judaism. The Committee works to educate the Temple community about the unique blessings and challenges encountered by interfaith families and individuals who have converted or are in the process of conversion.

Baderech Mentors

Baderech: The Mentor's Commitment

As indicated by the mission statement at the front of this Guide, the *Baderech* program is a mentoring program that offers encouragement, guidance and connections for the prospective convert/Choosing Judaism student through the assignment of a carefully matched mentor. Both the CJ student and the mentors fill out brief questionnaires that assist us as we "match" the student to his/her mentor.

The mentors for the *Baderech* program must attend the training session (1 ½ hours) provided by *Baderech* co-chairs Penny Coney and Amy Seals. The mentor is actively involved at Temple Emanu-El, possesses qualities important for mentoring, and has exhibited a commitment to Reform Judaism.

The conversion process time frame for each individual prospective convert/CJ student varies in length, but it is generally expected that the entire process will take at least 1 year. For this reason, the *Baderech* mentor makes a 1-year commitment to his/her assigned CJ student. During the year, the mentor assists the CJ student on his/her path of learning and engagement with the Temple Emanu-El community, with the goal of helping the CJ student find his/her spiritual home at Temple Emanu-El.

The interaction/relationship that develops between the mentor and CJ student is self-directed and nurtured, but with some general expectations outlined by the program (The Mentoring Year).

Questions about the *Baderech* program, including inquiries for participating as a mentor, may be directed to Penny Coney or Amy Seals, *Baderech* co-chairs, or Diana Coben Einstein, Associate Program Director, Temple Emanu-El.

The Mentoring Year

Congratulations—it's a match! You've been chosen as a mentor for a student in the Choosing Judaism class. Now what??

We're asking that you commit to mentoring your student for one year. During this year, the student will complete the Choosing Judaism class, work with a rabbi, and begin living a Jewish life within the Jewish community.

As a mentor you will be instrumental in linking your student to the opportunities for worship, learning, social justice, and fun Temple, and the larger Jewish community. You have a lot to offer! So here are some possible activities that can connect you and your student during this exciting year of learning and discovery.

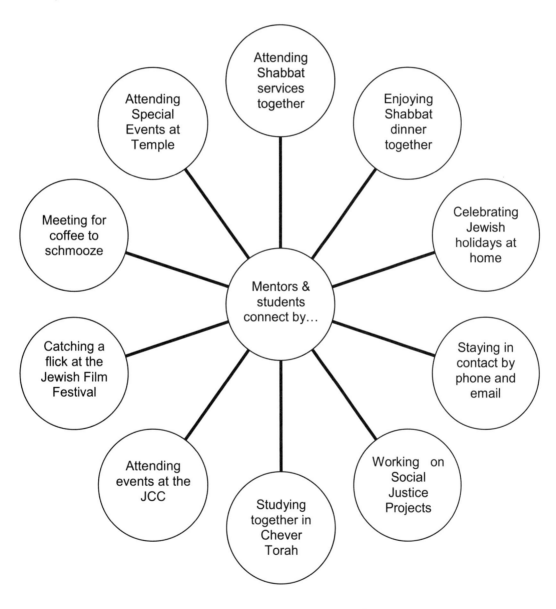

Mentor Profile

*The one who brings another
under the wings of the Divine Presence
is regarded as if he or she had created that person.*

Genesis Rabbah
(Lech L'cha 39:14)

Patient
Flexible
Positive
A learner
Pro-active
Supportive
Not perfect
Empathetic
Encouraging
Likes to laugh
A good listener
Non-judgmental
Open to questions
On a personal journey
Willing to seek answers

Chapter Three   Outreach   **107**

Choosing Judaism Student-Mentor Relationship Matching Questionnaire

Please choose one. I am a: ☐ CJ Student   ☐ Mentor

Name: _____   Email: _____

Phone: _____   Age: _____

Married ___ Single___ Divorced ___ Widowed ___

Child(ren) and age(s):

Occupation: _____

Hobbies: _____

CJ Student Only—Current involvement at Temple Emanu-El, if any:

The purpose of this questionnaire is to help us in our process of matching the CJ student to a mentor. The more information you can provide, the more helpful the questionnaire will be in our matching efforts.

CJ Students, please note: Specific preferences for your mentor (e.g., "I want a mentor who is married with young children"), will be discussed during your "*Baderech* Phone Interview" with a representative of the *Baderech* Program.

1. The area of Jewish life to which I am most drawn or most curious about is (e.g., cooking, worship, etc.):

2. One aspect of Judaism that I would like to learn more about is:

108   The Outreach and Membership Idea Book Volume III

3. Please use the space below to tell us if there is anything specific you are looking for in your mentor, or perhaps attributes you would prefer NOT to have. For example: "I would prefer a mentor who doesn't have young children" or "I would like someone who is open to same sex couples." All answers will be kept confidential.

4. The following is a list of potential activities for the CJ Student/Mentor to participate in together. Please indicate your preferences —"Yes" if you are interested, "No" if you're not interested, and "Maybe" if you might be interested. There is space at the bottom for you to add additional activities.

Yes	No	Maybe	Activity
			Meet on *regular* basis for coffee and conversation
			Meet as *desired* for coffee and conversation
			Attend Shabbat services
			Share Shabbat dinner
			Celebrate Jewish holidays
			Attend lectures and other programs at Temple
			Attend adult learning classes (e.g., Chever Torah)
			Cook together and exchange recipes
			Find/shop at Jewish stores
			Attend Jewish cultural events, such as plays, movies, museums
			Social Justice/volunteering
			Other (Please list any other activities in which you are interested.)

Baderech CJ Student Phone Interview Questionnaire

This questionnaire is to be used in conjunction with the Choosing Judaism Student-Mentor Relationship Matching Questionnaire, filled out by the CJ student.

Date_____

CJ Student_____

Baderech Rep* _____

(*Interviewer)

1. How is Choosing Judaism going?

2. Please share a little bit about yourself (where you're from, what kind of work you do, your family, etc.)

3. If you're comfortable, please share what brought you to consider converting to Judaism. (optional question)

110   The Outreach and Membership Idea Book Volume III

4. As you know, Temple Emanu-El is a big place with lots of opportunities for worship, learning and fellowship. How important is it to you to have a mentor that will:

_____ attend worship services with you

_____ attend lectures, workshops, etc at Temple with you

_____ invite you to share the Jewish holidays with them

_____ be available to meet with you on a regular basis

_____ provide "hands on", practical lessons (e.g., how to light Shabbat candles)

_____ Other

5. When thinking about who would be the best mentor match for you, would you prefer:

	Yes	No	No preference	Notes/Comments
Same gender				
Same Age *or*				
Older than you				
Same marital status				
Children of same age				
Similar interests				

6. Is there anything that would be a "deal-breaker" for you about a mentor? Such as:

Does not keep kosher

Smoker

Different sexual orientation than you

7. Can you think of anything else that will help us find the best mentor for you?

Guidelines for the Mentor:
Welcoming Your CJ Student and
Initiating the Mentoring Relationship

This list of guidelines is designed to help you "break the ice" and begin developing your relationship with your assigned CJ student.

1. As soon as you receive your CJ student's contact info, please call your CJ student to introduce yourself. Please do not delay in calling them.

2. Set up a "first meeting" with the student—we recommend meeting in a quiet place where you can talk easily. Suggestions for this first conversation:

   a. Have the student tell you about his/her life in general—a typical "first time meeting a person" conversation (job, family, hobbies, etc.). At this point, it's probably best not to get too involved in the "Why are you converting" discussion, unless they bring up the topic.

   b. Ask them if and how they are getting involved at Temple and/or the larger Jewish community.

   c. Find out what their interests are in terms of upcoming (within the next month) opportunities at Temple. You may want to have the current issue of the Temple Window with you. Their general interests will be provided to you, but you should ask them about specific events. Invite them to an event you know you will be attending.

   d. During your first conversation/meeting, reassure the student that you are there for them and that you will maintain confidentiality.

   e. At the end of the first meeting, decide when you will next talk or get together. Exchange additional contact info if needed (email address, for example).

3. Follow-up with the student in 2-3 weeks if you do not hear from him/her.

4. Attend the "*Baderech* Kick-Off Event," date/time TBA. (*Note: This may take place prior to your first meeting with your assigned CJ student.*)

Please contact us with any questions,

Amy Seals, sealsa@prodigy.net, 214-448-0277

Penny Coney, coneyL@cfbisd.edu, 972-971-3360

Outreach

Becoming a Jew
Questions and Answers

Each year in North America thousands of people convert to Judaism. While each person's path into Jewish life is unique, there are many shared questions. This page is intended to answer some of these basic questions and to point the way to additional sources.

1. Why do people consider converting to Judaism?

   There are many reasons. Often an interreligious marriage sparks an interest in the non-Jewish partner that can lead to a desire to share the religion of his or her spouse.

   Similarly, when an interfaith couple decides to raise children, the non-Jew may initially decide to explore Judaism in order to seek a religious common ground for the family.

   Other men and women seeking religious meaning in their lives, with or without any connection to a Jewish mate, find that Judaism offers them the best medium of religious expression.

2. Do Jews seek converts?

   Centuries ago, Jews did engage in proselytizing, particularly during the Graeco–Roman period of Jewish history, when thousands of non-Jews living in Asia Minor embraced Judaism. The destruction of the Roman Empire and mortal threats against Jews who sought converts marked the end of such efforts to gain converts.

   Judaism respects the religious beliefs of others, as well as the convictions of those who choose no religion. At the same time, Judaism is an open religion that readily accepts and encourages those who look to it for fulfillment and guidance in meeting life's c h a l l enges. In recent years, the Reform movement, through its Commission on Outreach and Synagogue C o m m u n i t y, has taken a more active approach to seeking out people who might choose to become Jews. (This pamphlet is an example of such an approach).

3. How do I know if Judaism is right for me?

   The best way is to learn as much as you can about Judaism and begin to practice those aspects of Judaism that most appeal to you. Seek out Jewish friends, Jewish family members, or a synagogue community for support. As you study and try out Jewish practice and customs at your own pace, you will become comfortable with them and prepare for further steps. An excellent way to get a sense of the traditions and practice of Judaism is to take an Introduction to Judaism course. The Reform movement sponsors these courses throughout North America.

4. If I take an Introduction to Judaism class, will I be expected to convert?

   No. These courses are offered to anyone who wants to learn more about Judaism.

   They are most often attended by individuals considering conversion, by interfaith couples learning together about Judaism and making decisions about whether to have a Jewish home, as well as by born Jews who want to learn more about their own heritage. Although many people do take the course as part of their process of choosing Judaism, there are no assumptions or expectations held about people taking the class.

5. If I decide that I want to become a Jew, how would I go about it?

First, make an appointment with a rabbi. The rabbi will not only discuss the process and implications of becoming a Jew, but also explore with you your reasons for wanting to do so. In earlier generations, rabbis would discourage potential Jews-by-choice, turning them away three times to test how serious they were. This custom is seldom followed today, but most rabbis still endeavor to impress upon the potential convert the seriousness of such a choice.

6. If I become a Jew, would people refer to me as a "convert"? Is there some other, more proper term to use?

In Judaism, people who become Jews have no less than full Jewish status in every circumstance. For this reason, there may be some objection to any distinctive term that refers to a person who has chosen to become a Jew. On the other hand, many people are proud to let others know they are converts to Judaism. Also, as the number of people becoming Jews continues to increase and as various Jewish religious institutions develop programs to encourage and assist people in this process, it has become useful to talk m o re publicly about choosing Judaism. Consequently, a number of terms have come into common usage, including "convert" and "Jew – by-choice," often used interchangeably. In our free society in North America today, however, Jewish commitment is a matter of choice for all who are Jews, by birth or conversion.

7. If I become a Jew, what would be the attitude of other Jews toward me?

Judaism has always welcomed those who voluntarily become Jews and considers them full-fledged members of the Jewish community. The Hebrew Bible, as well as later Jewish texts, includes examples of such individuals. The most famous and honored example appears in the biblical Book of Ruth, where Ruth joins the Jewish people and eventually becomes the grea t – grea t – grandmother of King David, from whose descendants, according to Jewish tradition, the Messiah will come. In our day, most Jews welcome wholeheartedly those who have chosen to become Jews. Nonetheless, some Jew s – by-choice re p o rt occasional offensive comments dire c t e d toward them. Although the reasons for such attitudes are complicated, they are based on ignorance and prejudice and are by no means sanctioned by Judaism. As more and more Jew s – by-choice enter the Jew i s h community, as Reform Jewish Outreach promotes education about Jewish views of conversion and sensitivity to Jews – bychoice, and as public discussion of such a choice grows more commonplace, these negative views will continue to fade.

8. If I convert with a Reform rabbi, will all rabbis consider me a Jew?
Reform, Re c o n s t ructionist, and, under certain circumstances, Conservative rabbis re c o g n i ze the validity of conve r s i o n s p e rformed by rabbis of all branches of Judaism. Many Orthodox rabbis, however, do not recognize non-Orthodox conversions.

Your sponsoring rabbi will be able to discuss further any implications for you of conversion under his or her auspices. People considering conversion are expected to study Jewish theology, rituals, history, culture, and customs and to begin incorporating Jewish practice into their live s. The scope of the course of study will vary from rabbi to rabbi and community to community. Most now require a course in basic Judaism and individual study with a rabbi, as well as attendance at services and

114   The Outreach and Membership Idea Book Volume III

participation in home practice and synagogue life. Keep in mind that you are free to choose the rabbi with whom you will work. Talk to more than one rabbi and find one with whom you are comfortable. This rabbi will then become your guide every step of the way through your conversion.

9. If I become a Jew, will I be expected to separate from my family of origin?

By no means. Most Jews-by-choice maintain warm relationships with their family of origin. Conversion to a new religion does not suddenly make you over into something altogether new; nor does it cut you off from old family ties or memories. However, some converts to Judaism find that, especially initially, their family may be hurt or confused by their choice. Such feelings often result from misunderstandings or a lack of knowledge about Judaism and are, therefore, perfectly understandable. If it happens with your family, what will help immensely is your patience, as well as a willingness to discuss your choice and to show your family that you've not abandoned them.

10. If I decide not to become a Jew but I have a partner who is, can our children be raised as Jews?

Yes. Many interfaith couples have decided to raise their children as Jews. In many families today, non-Jewish parents play a key role in providing for their childre n's Jewish education, as well as creating a supportive Jewish home environment. The more you learn about Judaism, the easier this will be for you. Many Jews see such parents as the givers of a precious gift and as a blessing to the Jewish people.

11. If I decide not to become a Jew, would I be welcome to worship in a synagogue with my Jewish family?

Most Reform and Reconstructionist and some Conservative and Orthodox congregations warmly welcome interfaith families to participate in various ways in synagogue life. In following the famous verse from the Book of Isaiah 56:7, "For My house shall be called a house of prayer for all peoples," almost all Jewish religious services are open to the public, so you and your family would be welcome to attend. Sabbath services are held on Friday evening and Saturday mornings. Call the specific congregation during the week to find out the times.

12. If I'm not yet ready to convert to Judaism or if I decide not to, what options do my Jewish partner and I have for our wedding ceremony?

This is a very sensitive issue, on which there is a broad range of opinions. We encourage you to seek out a rabbi with whom you feel comfortable and have a thorough discussion about the options. No matter what kind of wedding ceremony you have, Reform Judaism considers itself a portal to Jewish life for intermarried families. Through organized Ou t re a c h programming and a general atmosphere of openness, an interfaith couple will find a welcome at Reform congregations.

Union for Reform Judaism: Becoming a Jew: Questions and Answers

What Do I Do If I Am Faced With A Question I Can't Answer?

As a mentor, you will be offering guidance to the prospective convert/CJ student, which will result in a rewarding relationship! You've been invited to the *Baderech* program because you are knowledgeable, you are active at Temple Emanu-El, and you possess the necessary qualities for being a mentor.

But you may also be faced with a challenging question or issue from your prospective convert/Choosing Judaism student. Sometimes, the question/issue is so challenging, that you will feel that you just cannot provide the answer or guidance that the CJ student needs. What do you do? While some of the advice presented here is certainly obvious (therefore you probably don't even need a reminder of it!), we hope that outlining it here, as well as including some "not so obvious" strategies, will be helpful to you should you find yourself in the situation.

Following is an outline of "what to do" when faced with an especially challenging question or issue from your prospective convert.

1. First, *acknowledge the importance of the question or concern*. When a person is on the conversion journey, the possibilities for challenges from a variety of sources are quite diverse.

2. *Assure the CJ student that you want to help* him/her.

3. As obvious as it may seem, please do not make up an answer, or give advice that you are uncertain of. *Admit that you don't have an answer or advice*, but that you will help the CJ student find the answer or advice.

4. *Encourage the CJ student to talk to his/her rabbi* during one of their meetings. If the situation is urgent, and a meeting is not scheduled for the immediate future, the CJ student may wish to call his Choosing Judaism teacher as this person has a lot of experience guiding CJ students. Another alternative would be to call Diana Coben Einstein, who is Temple's Associate Program Director, and oversees the Conversion Program. The members of the Outreach Committee are also excellent sources of assistance and guidance. Finally, other chavers/mentors, especially those who have served in the past, may be experienced helping with the very same question/issue. Ask the student if you may talk to another mentor on their behalf, or if they prefer to talk directly, put them in touch with the other mentor. (See the Resources section of your *Baderech* Handbook for contact information.)

5. *Consult the Resources section* of your *Baderech* Handbook. If the specific answer is not there, you may find other sources that will lead you to the answer.

6. Finally, *follow up with the CJ student*, to see what has happened with the situation/question, and offer additional support.

Conversion Journey at Temple Emanu-El

Conversion to Judaism

***"The Holy One, Blessed be God, loves gerim (converts) greatly"* – Midrash**

Gerut (conversion) is a challenging and powerful process. While it requires strong dedication and soul-searching, the results are extraordinary. As Lydia Kukoff, herself a Jew-by-Choice, writes, "Those who choose Judaism are witnesses to the beauty and value of Jewish tradition."

At Temple Emanu-El, gerut follows a period of preparation of about a year in length. During this period, the prospective Jew-by-Choice studies about Judaism, participates in the life of the synagogue and the Jewish community, and develops and deepens his or her personal commitment to, and relationship with, God, Torah and the Jewish people.

We look forward to working with you as you explore Jewish life. For more information on conversion, please contact Diana Coben Einstein.

Conversion Contact Information

Diana Coben Einstein, Associate Program Director

(P) 214.706.0000 ext.126 | (E) deinstein@tedallas.org

Requirements for Conversion

Requirements for gerut at Temple Emanu-El include all of the following: Stepping Stones to Jewish Knowledge: A Basic Judaism Class If you are ready to:

take your first or next step to a Jewish life filled with knowledge

explore ways to build a Jewish home a strengthen your Jewish family

feel more comfortable with prayer and worship

connect with members of our congregation

know more about Reform Judaism, then

Stepping Stones to Jewish Knowledge: A Basic Judaism Class is for you!

Stepping Stones to Jewish Knowledge is divided into two separate courses making it easier and more convenient for you to get the knowledge that you need while adding this community building experience to your busy schedule.

Classes meet on Tuesday nights from 7:30-9:00 p.m. The cost for each course is $120 per person, which includes books and our extraordinary faculty, and requires advanced registration.

Stepping Stones to Jewish Knowledge I: Our Homes, Families and Community begins February 3rd. These eight sessions will be taught by Renee Karp and include a Shabbat dinner.

Stepping Stones to Jewish Knowledge II: Our History, Literature and Faith begins March 31st and will be taught by Robin Kosberg. These eight sessions include two Saturday sessions.

Both courses are a pre-requisite for those interested in conversion.

To register contact Nita White at 214.706.0000 ext. 131 or nwhite@tedallas.org. For more information regarding conversion, contact Associate Program Director Diana Coben Einstein at 214.706.0000 ext.126 or deinstein@tedallas.org.

Choosing Judaism – At the conclusion of Stepping Stones, "Choosing Judaism," our conversion program, will begin meeting several times a month for a total of eight sessions. This group, facilitated by trained lay leaders, will examine many of the personal issues that prospective Jews-by-Choice face with opportunities for reflection and sharing.

The Spring 2009 Choosing Judaism class dates are: January 27, February 10, February 24, March 10, March 24, April 7, April 28, and May 12. All classes will meet from 5:45 – 7:15 p.m. The cost for the class is $70.

The book list for the Choosing Judaism class is listed here. Books will be included in the cost of the class and will be provided to you in the first class.

- Living a Jewish Life, Updated and Revised Edition: Jewish Traditions, Customs and Values for Today's Families *by Anita Diamant*
- Choosing a Jewish Life: A Handbook for People Converting to Judaism and for Their Family and Friends *by Anita Diamant*
- Choosing Judaism *by Lydia Kukoff*
- Embracing the Covenant: Converts to Judaism Talk About Why & How *by Allan Berkowitz*

Jewish Living – The prospective Jew-by-Choice begins to "see the world through Jewish eyes" through the celebration of Shabbat and holidays, attendance at worship services and study sessions, observance of mitzvot, and participation in the Jewish community.

Tikkun Olam – Each prospective Jew-by-Choice will engage in ongoing acts of tikkun olam, helping to make the world a better place through donating their time in community service or social action projects.

Personal Reflection and Study – Individuals will complete the "Questions for Conversion" about Judaism and their beliefs during their conversion journey. In "Choosing Judaism" each person will complete a personal journal reflecting on their Jewish experiences for each group meeting. Candidates will also read a Jewish book and reflect on it for the final session.

Conferences – The sponsoring rabbi will have several individual meetings with the prospective Jew-by-Choice during the gerut process.

Outreach and Mentoring – Each student will be matched with a mentor who is a Temple member through our Baderech Program. Baderech is a Hebrew word meaning "On Your Path." Mentors will be a resource and friend to the prospective Jew-by-Choice during the conversion process. Students

118   The Outreach and Membership Idea Book Volume III

will call on them for any questions about Judaism, the conversion process, or attending services or programs at Temple.

Becoming a Member of Temple Emanu-El – Unless previous arrangements have been made with the rabbi, each candidate agrees to become part of the Temple Emanu-El Jewish community upon completion of gerut by joining this Temple as a member.

Gerut Ceremony – As the candidate prepares for conversion, the rabbi and candidate will discuss the opportunity to participate in the traditional rituals of mikvah (ritual immersion) and, as appropriate, ritual circumcision or hatafat dam brit (ritual circumcision). The gerut ceremony will take place in the Sanctuary or one of the chapels at Temple Emanu-El. The candidate will write a personal statement in preparation for this day. After the ceremony, all those new to Judaism are encouraged to be welcomed by the community at a Shabbat service and in the Temple Window.

A Sinai Sea of Jews By Choice

To commemorate the twentieth anniversary of Reform Jewish Outreach during Shabbat services at the UAHC Biennial in December, 1999, Jews by Choice were honored with an aliyah. Of the estimated 5,000 people who worshipped together, 300 ascended the bimah.

We were a few rising
Hesitant at first
Moving forward.
Then we were a stream
Flowing toward Torah.
We looked at each other
Surprise, overwhelmed;
We recognized ourselves
In the faces we saw
We were Jews By Choice.
The stream became a river.
We moved together
Up aisles of friends, teachers, lovers.
Up we flowed onto the bimah.
We were smiling weeping;
We knew each other
Though we had never met.
We stood amazed
Before the light
Of Torah
We looked around;
The river became a sea.
We were as numerous
As the crowd at Sinai;
We *were* the crowd at Sinai.
We are Jews By Choice.
We are a blessing,

A gift to the people Israel,
We felt it.
We belonged.
There, here.
We belonged to Torah
As Torah belongs to us.
We kept coming
This sea of Jews By Choice.
We said the blessing
Together, a Sinai sea strong.
Strangers who were not
Strangers anymore.
One of our own
Chanted Torah
We were proud.
We were a stream,
A river, a sea
Of Jews By Choice.
A stranger
Who was not a stranger
Wrapped me in her tallit.
We loved each other
We loved being Jews
We loved belonging.
We were called
And we came
This Sinai sea of Jews By Choice.

From Chametz to Rosh Hashanah

By Christina Ager

I am a Jew (by choice)
Who thought for one minute last week,
The week before Rosh Hashanah,
That I needed to put the chametz away
and buy matzah.
I have lived as a Jew for 5 years although officially for two (as if identity can ever be
officially bestowed).
I was ashamed, embarrassed by the error.
How could I?
Interesting: Not once, not even the very first year
Did I ever confuse Rosh Hashanah with Pesach.
Or vice versa.
And yet this year,
My first year as a Jew
I made that error: Chametz and Rosh Hashanah.
I am scared yet secure:
Secure:
I know I am a Jew, of that I have no doubt.
Scared:
How? How will I maintain it alone,
Separated from my family?
I have not the genetic background
To link me despite years of non-practice
Or three day Judaism (Rosh Hashanah, Yom Kippur, and Pesach)
To this people, this tradition.
Secure:
I am deeply committed.
Secure:
I have learned.
Scared:
Whenever I don't know something
I wonder, "Is it because I am a convert?
Does every other Jew know this?"
Secure:
Torah is study.
And so this High Holy Day,
This turning toward the New Year
I venture forth
Alone,
Yet not alone,
For years of tradition
Will carry me home
From Chametz to Rosh Hashanah.

Chapter Three   Outreach   **121**

Head Count

Friday night services at Congregation Emanu-El Israel (CEI) – the only synagogue in Greensburg, Pennsylvania – always began with a tradition that I suspect few even noticed. CEI, led by Rabbi Sara Perman, is a blended congregation, created when the Reform temple and Conservative synagogue realized that neither had the resources to continue alone. Even as one, they are a small congregation, filling only a few rows of their beautiful sanctuary. So each Friday night, I watched as Rabbi Perman took the count from the bimah, silently scanning the small clusters of congregants, determining if she had a minyan and would read Torah that night. More often than not, the answer was no.

I noticed because I knew that I didn't count. I was born and baptized Christian, conversion wasn't even on my radar at the time, and I was initially drawn to CEI because it seemed like the only place my wife could be comfortable in tiny Greensburg. It was nothing against me as a person; the congregation welcomed both Carla and me with a warmth and openness that I will never forget. I never held it against Sara either, who was a good friend as well as a good Rabbi, and who, perhaps unknowingly, built the foundation of my Jewish learning. Those were just the rules. I wasn't Jewish. Sure, I learned a lot of prayers on those Friday nights, minyan or no minyan, and I got quite good at following along – good enough that when we came to Des Moines, more than one person was surprised to learn that I wasn't Jewish. But no matter how well I passed, I was still pretending. I could fake my way along on rote memorization and transliterated Hebrew, but I didn't feel Jewish.

Potential converts, brace yourself. This should be the point of revelation, the happy story where I recount the exact moment where the big lightbulb came on, the fanfare of trumpets sounded, and just like that, I knew without a doubt that I was Jewish. Unfortunately, I don't have that story. Immersed in the mikveh, buoyed by its warmth, I couldn't wait to break the surface and begin a new life. Standing on the bimah, bearing the unexpected weight of the Torah scrolls, I had a brief glimpse of the opportunity that was being handed to me. And coming down off that bimah into the welcoming arms of family and friends, I knew I had made the right decision. But truth be told, the big light never came on. There are a lot of days I still feel like that uncounted fraud, playing along from the back rows in the Congregation Emanu-El Israel sanctuary, forcing awkward Hebrew words out of my mouth, turning the pages of the prayerbook the wrong way, still waiting for a revelation. Even the moment where I decided to convert, sitting in services on Rosh Hashanah (which now sounds staged, starting a new life for the new year, but that's when it happened) was an anticlimax. I simply looked around and asked myself, "What are you waiting for?"

According to the rules, I count now. Put me in a room with nine other Jews, you've got a minyan. I still stumble a bit in my new Jewish identity: can I really say "oy vey" with a straight face? And is gefilte fish really necessary? But I'm learning. And I'm just starting to realize that maybe the little anticlimactic question that started all this – what are you waiting for? – is the big lightbulb, the trumpet fanfare. Instead of waiting to feel Jewish, I'm trying (little by little) to be Jewish. And that's what counts.

Jews By Birth are Also Jews by Choice

When Does A Jew Become Jewish?

Recently at a Women of Temple Israel meeting, I asked for volunteers to mentor new converts and those in the process. Five people signed up. Ruth agreed to help then whispered in my ear that she is still sometimes referred to as Jew-by-Choice and it rankles her. She converted 25 years ago, teaches Hebrew, reads Torah, creates tallit and is a most knowledgeable and observant person. Most of the time I think of her as a companion at choir and study groups. When I think of her as a JBC, it is with wonder as I marvel at the way being Jewish is woven into the fabric of her life. Last year when she was called to read Torah for Yom Kippur, the Rabbi referred to her as a Jew-by-Choice in what he felt was a most complimentary way as he acknowledged the positive impact converts have made in our congregation. "When will I ever be just a Jew?" she asked.

As a Jew-by-Birth, but much more so as a Jew-by-Choice myself, I identify with her. Because my growing up years were in a huge classical reform congregation where I felt like a nobody who knew nothing, because we had no ethnic food at the table, because our Jewish journeys were to get Russian Rye down in the Fillmore, because I never joined BBGs [Jewish youth group] and because my family identified as Jewish but knew nothing about observance, because we were twice a year Jews and I always wanted more, because we had a Christmas tree until I was confirmed when my sister and I called a halt to that tradition and saddened my mother who just liked the smell and decorative aspects, because my husband is unobservant, doesn't want to go to temple and is a born Jew, because I've been on a steep Jewish learning curve, a spiritual quest for the past ten years, I am very much a Jew-by-Choice.

Ruth is in the midst of a sea change in Judaism. She's in her 40s-50s and she has no idea how typical she is in the Reform movement as congregations experience and work to support the diversity of their membership due to intermarriage and conversion. I can tell Ruth we are both Jews-by-Choice, but that doesn't make her feel any better or any more included. Somehow we all have to come to grips with the fact that what other people think or say reflects more about them than us. Probably feeling included is a personal journey in her life and she has lots of learning to do. Still, Ruth has been an observant Jew far longer than I have. We will always call people who convert something, and while we are cautioned against asking people why they have converted, I find their stories fascinating and they are happy to share their journeys.

Inclusion as an unhyphenated Jew continues to be a huge problem in Judaism on an even wider scale. I listened to a program on NPR recently about the Russian Jews, the law of return, "The Rabbis," and being treated as less than. Unless they came with pedigree papers, Russian Jews can't marry in Israel. No matter that they speak Hebrew, live a Jewish life, serve in the IDF. Their only option is to go through an Orthodox conversion. They have left one dictatorship to move to another and they won't go along a second time. So on the one hand they are returned and on the other they are still traife. When you are in the middle of a huge transition that may play out for decades, it's hard to feel you belong. Jewish Ruth, Russian Israeli Jews...what a strange situation for "the people" who have not been included throughout history. When you are in the middle of a huge transition that may play out for decades, it's hard to feel you belong."

Chapter Three   Outreach   **123**

Living A Jewish Life,
Living in the Jewish Community,
Self-Identifying as a Jew

How Do I Know When I'm Ready?

By Kathryn Kahn, Director of Outreach and Synagogue Community

In the days that formed the countdown to my marriage, I remember asking myself a series of anxious questions – a sort of final cross examination of my intentions on the eve of this most important ceremony that would, I hoped, begin a lifetime of commitment: Have I made the right choice? Am I sure of my feelings? Is this relationship the 'real thing'? Can it last a lifetime? Do I need more time to be sure? Am I ready? Asking these questions helped me to reaffirm the answers I already knew in my heart.

Twelve years after my marriage, I found myself asking similar questions on the eve of another equally important covenant – – my conversion to Judaism. In many ways the two covenants, to my husband and to Judaism, had the same essential elements – courtship leading to knowledge, love and public commitment. So how did I know I was ready to convert to Judaism? What are the essential elements that help insure the sincerity and authenticity of such an important decision?

Attraction to, and Knowledge of, the Beloved

When I first began to study about Judaism it was out of purely intellectual curiosity. Had anyone asked me then if I wanted to convert, I would have said, "Of course not!" There was no more deep personal commitment on my part than I would have had on a first date. Exploring Judaism is not the same as entering into the process of conversion. My studies were at first casual, wide-ranging and objective, but intriguing enough to me that I wanted to learn more. In effect, I was willing to 'go out again'! As time went on, I began to feel a deeper attraction, particularly for Judaism's ethical values. The ethics of Torah could only be brought to life by human acts—passive belief, unquestioning faith was not enough.

One essential element in becoming Jewish is "doing Jewish," whether by lighting Shabbat candles, arguing over the meaning of a verse from Deuteronomy, or attending a family seder. I was astounded when I found out that there was even a Jewish way to shop! According to our texts, if you do not plan on buying an item, you should not ask the store owner its price. He has to make a living and your idle curiosity is keeping him from attending to more serious customers! My interaction with Jews, in my husband's family and in the larger community, affirmed that same unique, profound approach to life and spiritual values. The more I discovered about Judaism, the more I wanted to know. That casual first "date" had led to a deepening relationship. After a year, I realized I had fallen in love with a religion, a people and a tradition.

Freedom from Other Attachments

A love relationship demands fidelity to the beloved. A commitment to a religion demands the same. My relationship with my birth religion had long ago ended and, although I respected my parents' beliefs and valued my background, it was no longer a part of me. I was free to embrace this unique and singular Jewish way of life, if I so chose.

Personal and Public Commitment

There is no such thing as a one-sided covenant in marriage or conversion. Each side commits to sacred obligations to nurture, to support, to pledge love and fidelity. This is no casual agreement. Because none of us can foresee the future, and because commitment is not only wonderful but awesome, many of us feel last minute uncertainties before we make momentous decisions in our lives. A conversion process that is long enough and profound enough will allow you to identify yourself as Jewish before the act of converting. It will carry you to that final ritual that will seem both right and inevitable. How will you know when you're ready? You'll know.

Personal Statement from Penny Coney

Well, what would my Southern Baptist grandmother think about this? How is it that the granddaughter of Alta Mae Ragsdale of Myrtle, Mississippi is standing before you today ready to become the daughter of Sarah and Abraham? Just like Sarah and Abraham is a family story, mine is too. You see Alta Mae and John Ragsdale had a daughter, Barbara, who grew up as a very good, no drinking, no smoking, no card playing, no dancing, Baptist girl. Then, she met Kirke Coney who grew up a good Methodist boy from a family that liked to smoke, drink, play cards and dance. To close the deal, he told her he'd become a Baptist *after* they got married. Hmmmm…..well, long story short they became Presbyterians.

Thus, my brother and I grew up in a home with smoking (until 1969), drinking, dancing and card playing. But, it was also a home where church was a very important part of our family. I believe I was it during second grade Vacation Bible School when I asked my mother, "we're doing Moses *again*?" Little did I know…

I thank my parents for giving me the gift of a religious upbringing that taught me that we are all God's children.

I am here today for many reasons, but not one of them is because I am unhappy with the way I was brought it. I am here today because this is where I fit. It is where my beliefs have found structure, where I have found a community, where I have found a way to talk to God and bring God into my life, where I've found a spiritual home.

And even though this home isn't the one my family imagined I'd find, they are happy I am no longer a nomad.

It is a mitzvah, a commandment, to honor your mother and father. That's an easy one for me – I honor you, I thank you, I love you for raising me up right, and still being there for me in the good times and the not so good times. Thank you to Ryan and Courtney for accompanying me on this journey….and now you have a Jewish mother….. I'm going to try to live up to that.

Thank you to my brother for all his love and support – he's not only a good brother, he's a real mench.

They say it takes a whole village to raise a child, well; it takes a whole Temple to raise a convert. Thank you to all my teachers – Renee, the two Connies, and poor Tom who still believes I'll eventually know the difference between a "kuf" and a "kof."

And of course, a special thank you to Rabbi Robbins for the guidance and inspiration I get from her each week in this chapel and especially for her support in preparing me for this day. Even though I share you with the whole congregation, you will always be "**my** rabbi."

I'd like to thank my fellow classmates who are here today; you have truly become wonderful friends. Thank you also to my Good Gator family and other friends that are here to help me celebrate.

In closing, I'd like to share comments from a sermon a rabbi was giving his congregation on Jews by Choice. He said "The greatest value of Jews-by-Choice in our congregation may be seen in an examination of this week's Torah portion. Moses sends scouts to report if the Land of Israel is a good one.

126 The Outreach and Membership Idea Book Volume III

Perhaps today's Jews-by-Choice are our scouts. They have scouted out the land, first as outsiders. They have looked at our faith; they have taken up our practices; they have joined our community; they have found Judaism to be good. Just as the scouts in the Torah found clusters of grapes so large that they had to be carried on a pole borne by two strong men, Jews by Choice have found our covenant to be fruitful. "

I find the covenant of Israel to be fruitful, and I am ready to say today that:

I accept Judaism to the exclusion of all other religious faiths and practices.

I pledge my loyalty to Judaism and to the Jewish people under all circumstances.

I commit myself to the pursuit of Torah and Jewish knowledge.

Welcome me, sons and daughters of Abraham and Sarah, for I am home.

Thank you

Chapter Three Outreach 127

Always there is a mountain in my vision…

If I try to recall a time in my life when there was no mountain in my vision, I am unable to.

For years, this mountain has been inspiring me to ask:

What is it?

What does it mean?

Why did the most spiritual moment I've ever had in my life-when I felt God's presence in the most profound way-literally take place as I gazed at a mountain?

Why, whenever I talk to God, or try to listen to God, do I always see this mountain?

So I have been seeking…

And I have reached *this* day after many years of walking down paths and retracing my steps,

After many contemplative nights of opening various books, and closing others,

After many moments discovering answers to some questions, while asking many more.

And every time I found the path that felt straight and true,

The book I wanted to keep open,

The answer that was clear and meaningful,

That path was Judaism.

That book was Torah.

The answer was my vision-my vision of the mountain.

Always there is a mountain in my vision.

And the mountain is Sinai.

-Amy Seals
Hannah bat Avraham v'Sarah
24 Cheshvan 5763
October 30, 2002

Resources

OUTREACH: THE CASE FOR A MISSIONARY JUDAISM

Address of
Rabbi Alexander M. Schindler
President
Union of American Hebrew Congregations

To the Board of Trustees
Houston, Texas
December 2, 1978

It is good to be here, my friends, good to be re-united with the leaders of Reform Jewry, with men and women from many congregations and communities but of one faith, bound together by a common sacred cause. Your presence here gives us much strength as does your work throughout the year. We are what we are because of you, a product of those rich gifts of mind and heart you bring to our tasks.

It is good to have our number enlarged by the presence of leaders and members of our Southwest congregations. We are grateful for your hospitality. You are true sons and daughters of Abraham whose tent, so the Midrash informs us, has an opening on each of its sides so that whencesoever a stranger might near he would have no difficulty in entering Abraham and Sarah's home.

We are grateful for the sustaining help which you have given us over the years, your material help, and the time and talents and energies of your leaders who have always played an indispensable role in our regional and national councils.

It is not my intention this night to give you a comprehensive report of the Union's activities—as I do at these Board meetings from time to time—but rather to offer a resolution which recommends the creation of an agency within our movement involving its every arm which will earnestly and urgently confront the problem of intermarriage in specified areas and in an effort to turn the tide which threatens to sweep us away into directions which might enable us to recover our numbers and, more important, to recharge our inner strength.

I begin with the recognition of a reality: the tide of intermarriage is running against us. The statistics on the subject confirm what our own experience teaches us: intermarriage is on the rise. Between 1966 and 1972, 31.7 percent of all marriages involving a Jew were marriages between a Jew and a person born a non-Jew. And a recent survey shows that the acceptance of such marriages among Americans in general is on the rise, most dramatically, as we might expect, among Jews.

We may deplore it, we may lament it, we may struggle against it, but these are the facts. The tide is running against us, and we must deal with this threatening reality. Dealing with it does not, however, mean that we must learn to accept it. It does not mean that we should prepare to sit *shiva* for the American Jewish community. On the contrary, facing and dealing with reality means confronting it, coming to grips with it, determining to reshape it.

Chapter Three   Outreach   **129**

Most often, Jewish education – more of it, and better – is put forward as the surest remedy to inter-marriage. And, indeed, there is some evidence that suggests that the more the Jewish education, the less the likelihood of intermarriage. But alas, it is not always so. As the Mishnah long ago averred, "Not every knowledgeable Jew is pious", not every educated Jew is a committed Jew.

Nonetheless, we believe in Jewish education, for its own sake as well as because we believe it a pow-erful defense against the erosion of our people. The bulk of the resources and the energies of the Union of American Hebrew Congregations is invested in programs of formal and informal education of which we are justly proud. We operate summer camps and Israel tours and youth retreats, college weekends and kallahs and teacher training institutes. We generate curricula and texts and educational aids. And some 45,000 youngsters participate each and every year in the programs, which we sponsor.

We know that such programs are our first line of defense in the battle against intermarriage. We know as well, however, that they are an imperfect defense, that even among those who are exposed to our most ambitious efforts, there are hundreds, if not thousands, who will intermarry. There is a sting to the honey of freedom.

But we know also that Jewish education is not "wasted" even on those who do intermarry. Study after study informs us that it is the Jewish partner of an intermarried couple who is most likely to determine whether or not there will be a conversion to Judaism, and whether or not the children of the couple will be raised as Jews. The richer the background and the stronger the commitment of the Jewish partner, the less likely is the absolute loss.

Most simply stated, the fact of intermarriage does not in and of itself lead to a decline in the Jewish population. As Fred Massarik, one of our leading demographers, has observed (MOMENT June 1978), "That decline – if a decline there be – depends on what the Jews who are involved in the intermarriage actually do."

As important as Jewish education is, in the context, I believe that there are other steps we can – and must – take if we are to deal realistically with the threat which intermarriage presents to our survival. And it is on three such steps that I want to focus my attention.

The first of these has to do with the conversion of the non-Jewish partner-to-be. It is time for us to reform our behavior towards those who become Jews-by-Choice, to increase our sensitivity towards them and, thereby, to encourage growth in their numbers.

In most communities, the UAHC offers "Introduction to Judaism" courses, and congregational rabbis spend countless hours providing instruction in Judaism. History and Hebrew are taught, ideas ex-plored, ceremonies described. But there, by and large, our efforts end. Immediately after the marriage ceremony, we drop the couple and leave them to fend for themselves. We do not offer them help in es-tablishing a Jewish home, in raising their children Jewishly, in grappling with their peculiar problems, in dealing with their special conflicts. More important still, we do not really embrace them, enable them to feel a close kinship with our people.

On the contrary: If the truth be told, we often alienate them. We question their motivations (since only a madman would choose to be a Jew, the convert is either neurotic or hypocritical). We think them less Jewish (ignoring that they often know more about Judaism than born Jews). Unto the end of their days, we refer to them as converts.

A colleague of mine recently received a letter from one who elected to become a Jew:

Dear_____ :

I know that I personally resent being referred to as a convert – a word that by now is alien to my heart. My conversion process was nearly ten years ago – I have been a Jew for a long time now. I think, eat and breathe Judaism. My soul is a Jewish soul though I am distinctly aware of my original background and birthright. This does not alter my identity as a Jew. If one is curious about whence I come or if indeed "am I really Jewish," the answer is categorically "Yes, I'm really Jewish – a Jew-by-Choice." I shall continue to grow and to search as a Jew. My "conversion process" was just that – a process which ended with the ceremony. From then on I was a Jew."

Such Jews-by-Choice have special needs and we need special guidance on how to meet those needs. What, for example, is to be done where a convert is more enthusiastic than his/her Jewish-born partner? And what of the past of the new Jew? He may have broken with the past, but in human terms he cannot forget, nor should he be expected to, his non-Jewish parents or family, and at special times of the year, say Christmas or Easter, he may well feel some ambivalence. And what of the difficult process through which one learns that the adoption of Judaism implies the adoption of a people as well as a faith, of a history as well as a religion of a way of life as well as a doctrine? May this not sometimes seem overwhelming to the new Jew?

It is time for us to stop relating to the new Jews as if they were curiosities, or as if they were superficial people whose conversion to Judaism reflects a lack of principles on their part, a way of accommodating to their partners-to-be. We should do that for their sake, and also for our own. For we need them to be part of our people. They add strength to us only if they are more than a scattering of individuals who happen to share our faith. Newcomers to Judaism, in short, must embark on a long-term naturalization process, and they require knowledgeable and sympathetic guides along the way, that they may feel themselves fully equal members of the synagogue family.

Let there be no holding back. It was Maimonides himself, answering a convert's query, who wrote:

You ask whether you, being a proselyte, may speak the prayers: "our God and God of our Fathers" and "Guardian of Israel who has brought us out of the land of Egypt," and the like.

Pronounce all the prayers as they are written and do not change a word. Your prayers and your blessings should be the same as any other Jew…This above all: do not think little of your origin. We may be descended from Abraham. Isaac and Jacob, but your descent is from the Almighty Himself.

* * *

I now come to the third and likely the most controversial aspect of the matter, I believe that the time has come for the Reform movement – and others, if they are so disposed – to launch a carefully conceived Outreach program aimed at all Americans who are unchurched and who are seeking religious meaning.

It would be easy to tip-toe here, to use obfuscatory language and be satisfied to hint at my purpose. But I will not. Unabashedly and urgently, I propose that we resume our vocation as champions of Judaism, that we move from passive acceptance to affirmative action.

No, I do not have in mind some kind of traveling religious circus. I envisage instead the development of a dignified and responsible approach. Let us establish information centers in many places, well-publicized courses in our synagogues, and the development of suitable publications to serve these facilities and purposes. In short, I propose that we respond openly and positively to those God-seekers whose search leads them to our door, who voluntarily ask for our knowledge.

I do not suggest that we strive to wean people from the religions of their choice, with or without the boast that ours is the only true and valid faith; I do not suggest that we enter into rivalry with all established churches. I want to reach a different audience entirely. I want to reach the unchurched, those reared in non-religious homes or those who have become disillusioned with their taught beliefs. I want to reach those seekers after truth who require a religion which tolerates – more than tolerates, encourages – all questions. I want especially to reach the rootless and the alienated who need the warmth and comfort of a people known for its close family ties, a people of ancient and noble lineage.

The notion that Judaism is not a propagating faith is far from the truth. It has been a practiced truth for the last four centuries, but it was not true for the forty centuries before. Abraham was a convert, and our tradition lauds his missionary zeal. Isaiah enjoined us to be a "light unto the nations" and insisted that God's house be a "house of prayer for all peoples." Ruth of Moab, a heathen by birth, became the ancestress of King David. Zechariah foresaw the time when men of every tongue would grasp a Jew by the corner of his garment and say, "Let us go with you, for we have heard that God is with you."

During the Maccabean period, Jewish proselytizing activity reached its zenith: schools for missionaries were established, and by the beginning of the Christian era they had succeeded in converting ten percent of the population of the Roman Empire—roughly four million people.

It is true that the Talmud insists that we test the sincerity of the convert's motivations by discouraging him, by warning him of the hardships he will have to endure as a Jew. But the Talmud also says that while we are "to push converts away with the left hand," we ought to "draw them near with the right."

After Christianity became the established religion of the Roman Empire, and later, again, when Islam conquered the world, Jews were forbidden to seek converts or to accept them. The death penalty was fixed for the gentile who became a Jew and also for the Jew who welcomed him. Many were actually burned at the stake, and the heat of the flames cooled our conversionist ardor. Even so, it was not until the 16th century that we abandoned all proselytizing efforts; only then did our rabbis begin their systematic rejection of those who sought to join us.

But this is America and it is 1979. No repressive laws restrain us. The fear of persecution no longer inhibits us. There is no earthly—and surely no heavenly—reason why we cannot reassume our ancient vocation and open our arms to all newcomers.

Why are we so hesitant? Are we ashamed? Do we really believe that one must be a madman to embrace Judaism? Let us shuck our insecurities; let us recapture our self-esteem; let us, by all means, demonstrate our confidence in the value of our faith.

For we live in a time when millions of our fellow-Americans are in search of meaning. Tragically, many of the seekers go astray, and some fall prey to cultic enslavement. Searching for meaning, they find madness instead.

132 The Outreach and Membership Idea Book Volume III

Well, Judaism offers life, not death. It teaches free will, not the surrender of body and soul to another human being. The Jew prays directly to God, not through an intermediary who stands between him and his God. Judaism is a religion of hope, not despair. Judaism insists that man and society are perfectible. Judaism has an enormous wealth of wisdom and experience to offer this troubled world and we Jews ought to be proud to speak about it, to speak frankly and freely, with enthusiasm and with dignity.

* * *

Following Rabbi Schindler's address, the Board of Trustees adopted *a resolution that created the Reform Movement's Outreach efforts.*

Excerpt from Sermon
by Rabbi Eric Yoffie at the Houston Biennial

Union for Reform Judaism
68th General Assembly
November 19, 2005 – Houston, TX

Let's talk now about welcoming of a very specific sort—welcoming non-Jewish spouses and converts to Judaism.

There is no better place to raise these issues than in Houston, for it was in this very city twenty-seven years ago that Rabbi Alexander M. Schindler initiated our Outreach program. He declared that we would not merely tolerate converts; we would enthusiastically embrace them. And he proclaimed that we would not sit shivah for our children who intermarry. This was not an endorsement of intermarriage, but rather a refusal to reject the intermarried. We would welcome them into our synagogues, our families, and our homes. We would do this in the hope that the non-Jewish partners would ultimately convert to Judaism; and if not, that they would commit themselves to raising their children as Jews.

The outreach revolution was Alex Schindler's greatest legacy to us and one of our Movement's greatest legacies to the Jewish world. It is, nonetheless, a revolution that remains unfinished.

To begin with, we need to do far more for the non-Jewish spouses in our midst. We welcome all such spouses, of course, including those who do not identify as Jewish. But when a spouse involves herself in the activities of the synagogue; offers support to the Jewish involvements of husband or wife; attends Jewish worship; and, most important of all, commits to raising Jewish children, he or she is deserving not only of welcome but of our profound thanks.

These spouses are heroes—yes, heroes—of Jewish life. While maintaining some measure of attachment to their own traditions, and sometimes continuing to practice their religion, they take on responsibilities that, by any reasonable calculation, belong to the Jewish spouse. And very often they do all of this without recognition from either their Jewish family or their synagogue.

I would like you to meet one such hero. Helen Dreyfus met Richard, her husband-to-be, on a blind date and later took an Introduction to Judaism class with him. Although she enjoyed the class and admired Judaism, she did not think that she could convert. But she and Richard agreed to raise their children as Jews and joined Temple Emanuel here in Houston. When her two boys started preschool, Helen felt embraced by the synagogue. Over time, much of the family's holiday and Shabbat preparation fell to her, and she grew to enjoy it. She also became involved in the Parent-Teacher Organization of the religious school. When her husband fell ill with colon cancer in 2003, Judaism was a source of consolation and the temple offered support throughout. Following Richard's death earlier this year, Helen and her sons—Daniel, 10, and Adam, 8—have remained immersed in religious school and temple life. I would like to ask Helen to stand.

Our obligation is to extend our appreciation with a full embrace to Helen and to others like her.

One way to express our thanks is with a formal ceremony of recognition. Some of our synagogues do this in a low-key way, perhaps at an annual breakfast meeting. Others choose a dramatic point in the liturgical cycle. Rabbi Janet Marder asks non-Jewish spouses to come to the bimah on Yom Kippur morning and then has the congregation stand as she blesses them with the *Birkat Kohanim*. Whatever approach we choose, surely we can agree on the need for every Reform congregation to recognize these remarkable individuals.

Another challenge that we face is the decline in the number of non-Jewish spouses who convert to Judaism. There is much anecdotal evidence to suggest that interest in conversion has waned in our congregations.

In the early years of Outreach, Alex Schindler often returned to this topic. Alex told us: "We need to ask. We must not forget to ask." And for a while, our Movement actively encouraged conversion. Many of our congregations began holding public conversion ceremonies during regular worship services, but such ceremonies are far rarer now.

The reason, perhaps, is that by making non-Jews feel comfortable and accepted in our congregations, we have sent the message that we do not care if they convert. But that is not our message.

Why? Because it is a mitzvah to help a potential Jew become a Jew-by-choice. Because the synagogue is not a neutral institution; it is committed to building a vibrant religious life for the Jewish people. Because we want families to function as Jewish families, and while intermarried families can surely do this, we recognize the advantages of an intermarried family becoming a fully Jewish family, with two adult Jewish partners. Judaism does not denigrate those who find religious truth elsewhere; still, our synagogues emphasize the grandeur of Judaism and we joyfully extend membership in our covenantal community to all who are prepared to accept it.

And by the way: Most non-Jews who are part of synagogue life *expect* that we will ask them to convert; they come from a background where asking for this kind of commitment is natural and normal, and they are more than a little perplexed when we fail to do so.

So we need to say to the potential converts in our midst: "We would love to have you." And, in fact, we owe them an apology for not having said it sooner.

Special sensitivities are required. Ask, but do not pressure. Encourage, but do not insist. And if someone says, "I'm not ready," listen. If we pursue conversion with a heavy hand, the result could be to generate resentment. And yes, there will be those for whom conversion will never be an option.

But none of this is a reason for inaction. The time has come to reverse direction by returning to public conversions and doing all the other things that encourage conversion in our synagogues.

There is one other Outreach issue that requires our attention.

It sometimes happens that when an identifying Jew marries an identifying Christian, the couple will bring both religions into the family. They tell themselves that "if one religion is good, then two religions are better." But what this does is cause confusion for a child, who recognizes at a very young age that he cannot be "both," and that he is being asked to choose between Mommy's religion and Daddy's religion. Virtually all psychological experts agree that interfaith couples should choose a single religious identification for their children. And the great majority of children in this situation report growing up lacking any sense of belonging. Nonetheless, some parents, desperate to avoid conflict with each other, insist on passing the conflict on to their children by asking them to decide for themselves. And they then enroll their child in both a Christian Sunday school and a Hebrew school, even though few can sustain two schedules of religious education.

Ten years ago, on the recommendation of our Outreach Commission, the Union Biennial passed a resolution encouraging our congregations to enroll only those children who are not receiving formal religious education in any other religion. This was a wise and a humane decision; still, some synagogues have been reluctant to comply. In some cases, they have adopted a "don't ask, don't tell" policy; even if a child is attending a church school, as long as the parents say nothing, the synagogue says nothing.

We understand the reasons for this reluctance. The Jewish parent, wishing to avoid conflict with a spouse's family, may feel that some Jewish exposure is better than none; and synagogue officials are reluctant to take steps that may alienate interfaith families. Nonetheless, there is no escaping that dual education is harmful and unfair to the child. It also causes problems in the religious school, where teachers are often unable to handle the conflicts that arise. Experience has shown that it is far better for our congregations to adopt our 1995 policy and present it in a sensitive way to all concerned. As our resolution stated, our Rabbis and educators should also meet with parents, explain the reasons for choosing a single religious tradition, and offer them study and counseling that will enable them to make this choice wisely.

True, it is difficult to formalize boundaries and to say "no," particularly for our Movement, which always prefers to open doors and build bridges. But sometimes it is necessary. Let us not forget the lesson of King Solomon, who—faced with two mothers claiming the same child—knew that the parent who refused to cut the child in half was the one who loved him more.

The Union's Department of Outreach and Synagogue Community has prepared a comprehensive guide to assist us in all of these areas: in recognizing the non-Jewish parents in our congregations; in inviting and supporting conversion; and in revisiting our resolution on religious school enrollment. By any accounting, our Outreach agenda is an ambitious one.

But so be it. In a little more than a quarter of a century, our Reform Movement has made the once radical idea of Outreach into a central pillar of Jewish life. In the process, we reached out to the affiliated and the unaffiliated, to the intermarried and the Jew-by-choice. And in so doing, we shared with others the beauty of Judaism and strengthened our destiny as a holy people. This is the legacy of Alex Schindler and we remain true to his vision.

NOTE FROM TEMPLE EMANU-EL OUTREACH COMMITTEE: If you would like more readings and information on the development of the Outreach movement within Reform Judaism in the United States, please contact Diana Coben Einstein, Associate Program Director.

URJ Outreach and Membership

Recommended Books and Web Resources on Judaism and Jewish Practice

INTERMARRIAGE

Friedland, Ronnie, and Edmund Case, eds. *The Guide to Jewish Interfaith Family Life: An InterfaithFamily.com Handbook*. Woodstock, VT: Jewish Lights Publishing, 2001.

Hyman, Meryl. *"Who Is a Jew?": Conversations, Not Conclusions*. Woodstock, VT: Jewish Lights Publishing, 1999.

Jacobs, Sidney J., and Betty J. Jacobs. *122 Clues for Jews Whose Children Intermarry*. Culver City, CA: Jacobs Ladder Publications, 1988.

Judson, Daniel, and Nancy H. Weiner. *Meeting at the Well: A Jewish Spiritual Guide to Being Engaged*. New York: URJ Press, 2002.

Keen, Jim. *Inside Intermarriage: A Christian Partner's Perspective on Raising a Jewish Family*. New York: URJ Press, 2006.

King, Andrea. *If I'm Jewish and You're Christian, What Are the Kids?* New York: URJ Press, 1993.

Kushner, Lawrence. *Jewish Spirituality: A Brief Introduction for Christians*. Woodstock, VT: Jewish Lights Publishing, 2001.

Petsonk, Judy, and Jim Remsen. *The Intermarriage Handbook: A Guide for Jews and Christians*. New York: Harper Paperbacks, 1991.

CONVERSION/CHOOSING JUDAISM

Berkowitz, Allan L., and Patti Moskovitz, eds. *Embracing the Covenant: Converts to Judaism Talk About Why & How*. Woodstock, VT: Jewish Lights Publishing, 1996.

Diamant, Anita. *Choosing a Jewish Life*. New York: Schocken Books, Inc., 1998.

Dubner, Stephen J. *Choosing My Religion: A Memoir of a Family Beyond Belief*. New York: Harper Perennial, 2006.

Epstein, Lawrence J. *Questions and Answers on Conversion to Judaism*. Northvale, NJ: Jason Aronson, Inc., 1998.

Homolka, Jacob, and Seidel Homolka. *Not By Birth Alone: Conversion to Judaism*. Edited by Walter Jacob, Esther Seidel, and Walter Homolka. London: Cassell, 1997.

Kessel, Barbara. *Suddenly Jewish: Jews Raised As Gentiles Discover Their Jewish Roots*. Lebanon, NH: University Press of New England, 2007.

Kukoff, Lydia. *Choosing Judaism*. Rev. ed. New York: URJ Press, 2005.

Lester, Julius. *Lovesong: Becoming a Jew*. New York: Arcade Publishing, 1995.

Myrowitz, Catherine Hall. *Finding a Home for the Soul: Interviews with Converts to Judaism*. Northvale, NJ: Jason Aronson, Inc., 1995.

Romanoff, Lena. *Your People, My People: Finding Acceptance and Fulfillment as a Jew by Choice*. 2nd ed. Identity Plus, 1999.

Chapter Three Outreach

INTRODUCTION TO JUDAISM AND JEWISH LIVING

Cohen, Henry. *What's Special about Judaism?* Philadelphia: XLibris, 2006.

Diamant, Anita, and Howard Cooper. *Living a Jewish Life: Jewish Traditions, Customs and Values for Today's Families*. Rev. ed. New York: HarperCollins Publishers, 2007.

Einstein, Stephen J., and Lydia Kukoff. *Every Person's Guide to Judaism*. New York: URJ Press, 1989.

Hertzberg, Arthur, and Aron Hirt-Manheimer. *Jews: The Essence and Character of a People*. New York: HarperOne, 1999.

Heschel, Abraham Joshua. *The Sabbath*. New York: Farrar, Straus and Giroux, 2005.

Jacobs, Sidney J. and Betty J. Jacobs. *Clues About Jews for People Who Aren't*. Culver City, CA: Jacobs Ladder Publications, 1991.

Kertzer, Morris N. *What Is a Jew?* Revised by Lawrence Hoffman. New York: Touchstone, 1996.

Knobel, Peter, ed. *Gates of the Seasons: A Guide to the Jewish Year*. New York: CCAR Press, 1996.

Kushner, Harold. *To Life! A Celebration of Jewish Being and Thinking*. New York: Grand Central Publishing, 1994.

Magida, Arthur J. *How to Be a Perfect Stranger: A Guide to Etiquette in Other People's Religious Ceremonies*. Vol. 2. Woodstock, VT: Jewish Lights Publishing, 1999.

Maslin, Simeon J., ed. *Gates of Mitzvah: A Guide to the Jewish Life Cycle*. New York: CCAR Press, 1979.

Perelson, Ruth. *An Invitation to Shabbat: A Beginner's Guide to Weekly Celebration.* New York: URJ Press, 1997.

Prager, Dennis, and Joseph Telushkin. *The Nine Questions People Ask About Judaism*. New York: Touchstone, 1986.

Sandmel, David F., Rosann M. Catalano, and Christopher M. Leighton, eds. *Irreconcilable Differences? A Learning Resource for Jews and Christians*. Boulder, CO: Westview Press, 2001.

Schulman, Zell. *Let My People Eat! Passover Seders Made Simple*. San Francisco: John Wiley and Sons, Inc., 1998.

Shapiro, Mark Dov. *Gates of Shabbat: A Guide for Observing Shabbat*. New York: CCAR Press, 1996.

Sonsino, Rifat, and Daniel B. Syme. *Finding God: Ten Jewish Responses*. Rev. ed. New York: URJ Press, 2002.

Steinberg, Milton. *Basic Judaism*. Harvest Book, 1965.

Syme, Daniel B. *The Jewish Home: A Guide for Jewish Living*. Rev. ed. New York: URJ Press, 2003.

Telushkin, Joseph. *Jewish Literacy Revised Ed.: The Most Important Things to Know about the Jewish Religion, Its People, and Its History*. New York: William Morrow and Company, 2008.

Washofsky, Mark. *Jewish Living: A Guide to Contemporary Reform Practice*. New York: URJ Press, 2001.

JEWISH PARENTING/GRANDPARENTING

Danan, Julie Hilton. *The Jewish Parents' Almanac*. Northvale, NJ: Jason Aronson, Inc., 1997.

Diamant, Anita. *The New Jewish Baby Book*. Woodstock, VT: Jewish Lights Publishing, 1994.

Diamant, Anita, and Karen Kushner. *How to Be a Jewish Parent.* New York: Schocken Books, Inc., 2000.

Doades, Joanne. *Parenting Jewish Teens: A Guide for the Perplexed.* Woodstock, VT: Jewish Lights Publishing, 2007.

Freedman, E. B., Jan Greenberg, and Karen A. Katz. *What Does Being Jewish Mean?: Read-Aloud Responses to Questions Jewish Children Ask About History, Culture, and Religion.* New York: Fireside, 2003.

Kushner, Harold. *When Children Ask About God: A Guide for Parents Who Don't Always Have All the Answers.* New York: Schocken Books, Inc., 1995.

Levin, Sunie. *Mingled Roots: A Guide for Grandparents of Interfaith Children.* New York: URJ Press, 2003.

Mogel, Wendy. *The Blessing of a Skinned Knee: Using Jewish Teachings to Raise Self-Reliant Children.* New York: Penguin, 2001.

Wolpe, David. *Teaching Your Children About God: A Modern Jewish Approach.* New York: Harper Perennial, 1995.

BOOKS FOR CHILDREN

Abraham, Michelle Shapiro. *Good Morning, Boker Tov.* New York: URJ Press, 2001.

Abraham, Michelle Shapiro. *Good Night, Lilah Tov.* New York: URJ Press, 2001.

Abraham, Michelle Shapiro. *Shabbat Shalom!* New York: URJ Press, 2003.

Gellman, Marc, and Thomas Hartman. *How Do You Spell God?* New York: HarperTrophy, 1998.

Kress, Camille. *Let There Be Lights!* New York: URJ Press, 1997.

Kress, Camille. *A Tree Trunk Seder.* New York: URJ Press, 2000.

Kushner, Lawrence, and Karen Kushner. *Because Nothing Looks Like God.*

Woodstock, VT: Skylight Paths Publishing, 2001.

Older, Effin. *My Two Grandmothers.* New York: Harcourt Children's Books, 2000.

Sasso, Sandy Eisenberg. *God's Paintbrush.* Woodstock, VT: Jewish Lights Publishing, 1992.

Seidman, Lauren. *What Makes Someone a Jew?* Woodstock, VT: Jewish Lights Publishing, 2007.

Outreach Contacts:
Baderech Co-Chairs

Amy Seals
214-448-0277
seals@prodigy.net

Penny Coney
972-971-3360
coneyl@cfbisd.org

Outreach Committee Co-chairs

Amy Seals
214-448-0277
seals@prodigy.net

Jane Larkin
972-735-8954
jane@larkinhf.com

Diana Coben Einstein, Associate Program Director
214-706-0000 x.126
deinstein@tedallas.org

Celebrating Our Diversity

Name of Congregation:	Leo Baeck Temple
Address:	1300 N. Sepulveda Blvd., Los Angeles, CA 90049
Phone number:	(310) 476-2861
Contact's Name and E-mail:	Amandell@leobaecktemple.org
Number of Member Units:	700 temple members
URJ District:	West District
Rabbis:	Rabbi Kenneth Chasen, Rabbi Leah Lewis
Outreach/Membership Chairperson:	Elizabeth Jacobs

Brief Description: Leo Baeck Temple has a number of families with one Jewish spouse or with children who have been adopted from Asia. Chinese New Year has become a Jewish event that has taken all of the joy and essence of the traditional Chinese New Year celebration and made it comfortable for both traditions. This event features an informal Chinese dinner, special activities celebrating overlapping histories of two magnificent traditions, and a rare and wonderful opportunity to see an authentic Chinese Lion Dance. During the event there are activity books for the children, a thirty-minute lesson on how to speak Mandarin, and an opportunity for families to share stories and traditions. In addition to all of this programming, we have invited our regional URJ Outreach and Membership director to come and present a workshop about diversity in Judaism. The program book includes information about the Jews of Keifeng and some Hebrew definitions including the name of the year (e.g., rat = *achb'rosh*).

Program Goal: Our goal is to broaden our community's cultural awareness. Our temple has twelve children of Chinese ancestry enrolled in our education programs. It is our hope that all of our temple families will join with us in celebrating the overlapping histories of two magnificent traditions, as well as the richness and diversity that resides within the words "Jewish identity." We would also love to be known as the congregation that welcomes families from many diverse backgrounds.

Target Population: All members of the temple were invited, especially families that have children. We also welcomed Jewish–Asian interfaith couples in the community.

Number of Participants: We have approximately 100–150 participants.

Number and Length of Session: This is a two-hour event held once a year.

Staffing Required: One point person on the temple's professional team, one assistant, one Mandarin teacher.

Total Cost of Program: $500.00 for Chinese Lion Dancers

$10.00 per person for the Chinese Buffet

$103.00 for decorations

Fee for Attendees: $18.00 for Adults

$10.00 for Children (12 and under)

Materials Needed:
- Chinese decorations, lions, pineapple, decorated Chinese lanterns, and pictures of the animal of the year
- Red envelopes, a tradition of Chinese New Year, are customarily given to children and other loved ones, and are filled with "lucky money" for a prosperous New Year and chocolate in the shape of coins. In the effort to fuse our traditions, our red envelopes are filled with the traditional chocolate coins instead of money and include "coupons for mitzvot."
- Kosher chocolate coins
- Brochure highlighting different families of the synagogue with connections to China, Chinese/Jewish coloring/activity book
- Television/DVD player and the *Scooby Doo* episode Seson 3, Episode 9: "Block-Long Hong Kong Terror"

Room Setup: Depending on how many people RSVP, we usually have about ten round tables with chairs.
- Tables are set up for the buffet meal.
- The decorations are placed on the walls and all over the tables.
- A place is set for each person.
- There is a red envelope at each place setting.

Childcare: This is a family program. Children of all ages are encouraged to attend; therefore, childcare is not necessary.

Refreshments: We offer a Chinese dinner buffet as the main sustenance for the evening.

Instructions to Facilitator: This can be a big event; it is very important that you have a committee that is willing to take on responsibility. As a facilitator, you need to be able to delegate responsibility to your committee chairs. Start by talking to the families that are of Chinese descent or have children from China to see if they would like to participate as a chair or on the committee of this event. Local lion dance troupes may get booked early, so it is important to book them as soon as you know the date of your event. Check in with your committee via e-mail or conference calls to ensure things are running smoothly.

Evaluation of Program: We only have anecdotal evidence of the success of this program. The families who created the program were thrilled and honored. Congregants came in large numbers to support the event and people were smiling and had a good time.

Follow-up: The program was very successful, growing every year. We hope to be able to offer this program every year as long as there is lay support.

Chapter Three   Outreach   **141**

social action at lbt

mitzvah of the month...**january**

we are collecting
warm sweaters, coats, scarves,
gloves and hats

These items will be used by
OPCC

OPCC, formerly the Ocean Park Community Center – is the largest and most comprehensive provider of services on the Westside of Los Angeles to low income and homeless youth, adults and families, battered women and their children, and people living with mental illness.

If you would like to get involved in the
MITZVAH of the MONTH PROGRAM please contact:
Rabbi Leah Lewis at 310.476.2861 or llewis@leobaecktemple.org or
Allison Lee, Monthly Mitzvah Coordinator at 310.472.7496
allisonlee@adelphia.net

chinese new year celebration
Thursday, January 29   6:00-8:00pm

Please join us for LBT's festive Chinese New Year celebration - this year at AJU!
This event will feature an informal Chinese dinner, special activities celebrating the overlapping histories of two magnificent traditions, and . . . a rare and wonderful opportunity to see an authentic Chinese Lion Dance without driving downtown. The entire LBT community and members are welcome to this event, which promises to be an evening not to miss!
RSVP by Monday, January 26 to the temple office at 310.476.2861 or matthew@leobaecktemple.org.
Adults $18 | Children (twelve and under) $10

---

social action at lbt

mitzvah opportunities this month...

sova food pantry tour

**Spend a Morning at SOVA on Sunday, January 11
9:30am - 12:00pm**

WHAT IS SOVA ALL ABOUT?
Where is the main SOVA warehouse? What does it look like? Who is eligible to apply to SOVA for assistance? How do they decide who gets what? Does SOVA provide other services, and if so, what are they? How often and for how long can a client receive food and services from SOVA? INQUIRING MINDS WANT TO KNOW! Don't you?

Wouldn't you like to see where you food donations go, and see how they are disseminated?

Sign up now to take a tour of SOVA's main pantry site on Sunday January 11, from 9:30am -12:00 noon. It promises to be interesting and informative. And, while you are there, perhaps you'll even get an opportunity to perform a little mitzvah stocking shelves, etc.
Space is limited to 20, so RSVP as soon as possible!
E-mail Marcie Medof at mmedof@aol.com or call her at: 818.344.5597.

---

social action in the community

sova food pantry

At LBT, there are many effective ways that we, as Jews, can work toward our communal goal of *Tikkun Olam*. Donating food to the SOVA Food Pantry is certainly one of the easiest! Each month a new food staple will be featured. Donations may be dropped off

Food of the Month
JANUARY:
CANNED SOUP
ALL items are happily accepted!

in the bins near the Religious School's "C" building or at the Early Childhood Center.

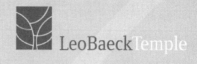

2009

leo baeck temple
**chinese new year
celebration** January 29, 2009
4707 | the year of the ox

Chapter Three   Outreach   **143**

Leo Baeck Temple
Chinese New Year Celebration

Thursday, January 29, 2009

4707 – the year of the ox

About the Red Envelopes

Red envelopes, a tradition of Chinese New Year, are customarily given to children and other loved ones and are filled with "lucky money" for a prosperous new year and candy in the shape of chocolate coins. In an effort to fuse our two traditions, our red envelopes are filled with the traditional coins and, instead of money, "coupons" for mitzvot. In the Jewish tradition, "mitzvot" (the plural of "mitzvah") are good deeds as well as holy "commandments." For our "mitzvot coupons," we have selected mitzvot involving good deeds that families and loved ones may perform together.

About the "Motzi" and the "Birkat HaMazon"

The Motzi and Birkat HaMazon, are, respectively, prayers of gratitude said before and after a meal. This evening, the Chinese-Jewish children of our planning committee will lead the motzi before our Chinese Buffet Dinner. Because the Birkat is often said silently for ordinary meals, but traditionally chanted out loud at festival gatherings, we invite all to join us this evening in the Birkat.

welcome

From the Event Committee

Tonight, as traditional Chinese Lion Dancers romp through the AJU's dining hall and as our children lead us in motzi followed by new year greetings in both Cantonese and Mandarin, we hope that you experience a thoroughly enjoyable evening. It is also our hope that you will join with us in celebrating the overlapping histories of two magnificent traditions, as well as the richness and diversity that reside within the words, "Jewish identity."

Several centuries ago, the Italian explorer Marco Polo recorded the presence of Jews in China. Archaeological evidence suggests that Chinese Jewish communities originated much earlier, with the migrations of Jews who traveled through Persia following the capture of Jerusalem in the first century CE. Historical records document the construction of a Jewish synagogue at Kaifeng in 1163, and a fifteenth century stele commemorates that Jewish soldiers and army officers served their Chinese homeland with "boundless devotion."

In more modern times, Jewish refugees found sanctuary from the Holocaust in Shanghai, where their community would later inspire the documentary, "Port of Last Resort" and the oral histories compiled by award-winning broadcast journalist Susan Stamberg. These refugees in fact formed a "second wave" of Jewish immigrants to Shanghai, where, a century before, Jewish settlers arriving from Baghdad and Bombay organized the Beth-El Synagogue.

In our own lifetimes, we have come together as members of two flourishing and industrious diasporas, communities who have made countless contributions to the art and science of contemporary society, while continuing to cherish and maintain their ancient traditions. We are all the daughters, sons, and grand-children of people who, in the last century, learned first-hand that the modern world could be a place of unspeakable cruelty as well as a place of unlimited possibilities for progress, discovery, and friendship.

As we come together to celebrate our two traditions, we are delighted and honored that so many of you have joined us. We wish you every blessing and a joyous new year.

Angela J. Davis
(Committee Chair)

Emily Brecher
陳陸良

Susan Sheu

Hanna Wernick
張航

Chapter Three   Outreach

reflections on jewish and chinese identity

The Colker / Sheu Family: Susan, Camille, Calvin, and Brian.

the colker/sheu family

by susan sheu

My father was Chinese, born in Fujian, China, and raised in Taipei, Taiwan. He and my mother, a Wisconsin native of Swedish and German origins, were among the first generation of intermarried couples in the United States. I was raised in a small city in Wisconsin in the 1970s and 1980s, where the only other Asians to be found were a small population of Hmong people from Southeast Asia. Although I never experienced overt racism, I was always aware of being perceived as different by most people I knew. Perhaps this was one of the reasons I was initially drawn to another very small group of kids in town, the Jewish ones, who all became friends. My first Jew-by-choice acquaintance was the father of a friend from high school, who had converted just before marrying his wife.

Conversion was not new to my family. My father and his family had converted from Buddhism to Christianity in China in the 1940s. Judaism appealed to me on many levels, and when I went to college in suburban New York, I had the opportunity to explore it through friendships and religion courses. When I later married a friend from college, I decided to convert to his religion, Judaism. The blending of our heritages in our family has been slanted toward mainstream American and Reform Jewish traditions, and we have visited our family in Taiwan and hope to stay in close touch. In Los Angeles we feel particularly at home because we are situated on the Pacific Rim in a community where we are no longer the exception.

The Wernick Family: Tiffany, Amanda, Hanna and Bruce.

the wernick family

by hanna wernick

This Chinese New Year we should celebrate the many similarities between the Jewish and Chinese cultures. My husband, Bruce, is proud to be a Jew and Sichuan Nishi (son-in-law). I love my "Yiddish Mama."

We are kindred spirits with similar values and traditions, and compatible in so many ways.

For example, the Chinese enjoy won ton soup. Jews enjoy matzah ball soup. Chicken noodle soup is universal and a source of comfort for all.

We celebrate Hannukah with gelt. The "red pocket" (hong bao) is the gift of choice for Chinese New Year (all right - Jews lose that one - The Red Pocket is filled with *real* money).

The Jewish and Chinese value education, charity, and a solid work ethic. Not that we don't share some eccentricities... (okay, maybe Jews are a little crazier).

The essence and core of Jewish and Chinese life is family. We are close knit and devoted to all generations, with compassion and caring.

Oh, lets not forget *mah jongg*!

Enjoy the Chinese New Year! The Year of the Ox. - Bruce, Hanna, Amanda & Tiffany Wernik

page 4

reflections on jewish and chinese identity

by emily brecher

When Avram asked me if I could help with the Chinese New Year celebration at Leo Baeck Temple, I thought what a great way to celebrate the two cultures. Being Chinese, born in Hong Kong, and married to a nice Jewish boy from Philadelphia, our family has been celebrating the two cultures since our wedding almost fifteen years ago.

Our wedding was a marriage of cultures. We were married by a rabbi under a *chupah*, my husband stepped on the glass and we had the chair dance. I thought for sure I was going to fall off from the chair. I changed into a traditional red Chinese dress, and my husband and I knelt down before my parents and my Jewish in-laws at the tea ceremony. The dim sum hors d'oeuvres were a huge hit. Our union of the two cultures went deeper than the practice of Jewish and Chinese customs. My husband and I found that the Jewish and Chinese cultures are very similar – the emphasis of family life, the importance placed on education, strong work ethics, and of course, we show our love through food.

We decided early on that we would bring up our children Jewish. Lucas had a *bris* and Sarah had a baby naming. We celebrate Passover, Hanukkah and Rosh Hashanah with our Jewish relatives. While giving our children a strong sense of Jewish identity, we celebrate the Chinese culture as well. We eat Chinese food often (my son would say too often); Sarah has traditional Chinese dresses; and I bring Chinese New Year to my children's classrooms with red packets and Chinese stories. Our visit to Hong Kong and China two years ago gave them an opportunity to experience the Chinese culture first hand.

My children recognize themselves as Jewish children of a Chinese mother. They do not see a conflict between their faith and their heritage. They attend Hebrew school here at Leo Baeck and will complete their Jewish rite of passage at their bat / bar mitzvah. When I told my 11 year-old son that there will be a Chinese New Year celebration at the temple, the event almost seems "natural" to him. His comment was, "We belong to a temple that is fun". How comforting is it that we belong to a temple that Jews of all cultures are accepted and welcome. Tonight, not only are we here to celebrate Jews from Chinese culture, we are here to celebrate Jews of all cultures – may they also find a place as welcoming as Leo Baeck Temple.

The Brecher family at the Great Wall of China. (2005)

Dressed in red, holding red packets for Chinese New Year. (center - 2001)

The Brecher Family - Emily, David, Lucas and Sarah. (bottom - 2008)

the brecher family

page 5

Chapter Three Outreach   **147**

reflections on jewish and chinese identity

by angela j. davis

In the late summer of 2003, I wrote to Rabbi Chasen to apologize that our family would not be attending the High Holy Day services that year, during which he would be officiating for the first time as the Senior Rabbi of Leo Baeck Temple. As my letter would go on to explain, we had an excellent excuse: our family had just received "The Phone Call," informing us that the Chinese baby girl for whom we had waded through what seemed like an infinity of foreign, international, and domestic bureaucracy, was now ready and waiting for us. We would be taking the midnight flight from LAX to Guangzhou before proceeding two days later to Chengdu, a city of 11 million people at the end of the Tibetan mountain plane. We would need to remain in China for fourteen days and would have time to see the famed "Big Buddha," as well as the world's largest panda preserve. We would be leaving in three weeks.

Of course, Rabbi Chasen understood and gave us his blessings. It was my impression that his words of congratulation were imbued with a special warmth because, as it happened, one of his most devoted Friday night worshippers was an irresistible little Chinese girl who would soon become a big sister. My daughter Chloe, who was four at the time, had joined our family three years earlier in Guanzhou, not far from the place of her birth. She first attended services at Leo Baeck when was she was barely three (with Rabbi Ragins) and could not stop talking about the magical place where she sat with rapt attention because "the rabbit was talking." (She insisted that Rabbi Ragins was a "rabbit," not rabbi, and her certainty took on a sort of uncanny, spiritual insight. When we traveled through Italy later that summer, each time we passed the grand cathedrals, she would tell me, with authority, "Mommy, that's a place that has rabbits talking inside.") As she grew older, she insisted that the family attend Friday night services, even to the point of tears if we dared suggest a quiet Shabbat entirely at home.

When Miranda joined our family, we soon realized we had to contend with two under-forty-pound leaders of the Friday night LBT services fan club. One summer week, after a short family trip to Monterey, the girls remembered over crepes and lemonade that the next day was Friday. "Will be home in time for Shabbat services?" was the big question after the glow of the Monterey Bay Aquarium's famed sting rays and jelly fish had begun to dim. We reminded them that it was a long drive, that we were *on vacation*, and that we could have a lovely Shabbat at home, or, for that matter, away from home. "With ice cream," my husband chimed in. To no avail. Some thirty hours later, after we had acquiesced to Highway 5 on a Friday afternoon in order to be at Getty Center Drive by 7:00pm, we realized when we passed the Laval Road

the rochmes / davis family

page 6

reflections on jewish and chinese identity continued

grapevine exit at about 6:30, that . . . it was simply not going to happen. "Girls," I began matter-of-factly, "there's been a lot of traffic and we had a really nice day in Monterey. We're probably not going to make it to services tonight." A roar of tears ensued. Suggestions of late night cocoa and cookies were met with closed eyes and shaking heads. Only the promise that they could write a little note to the clergy (combined with the renewed offer of cookies and cocoa) would calm the waters. It is perhaps surprising – but not *that* surprising – that our daughters were so magnetically drawn to Shabbat services at such an early age. The Friday evenings that they spent at Leo Baeck while very young gave them a very visceral (if unarticulated) sense of so many things that we, as adults, find so elusive in our contemporary lives: a sense of a sacred time, when their parents did not speak about work and tried to avoid their email accounts; a feeling of quiet and sanctuary that was beyond rational argument (or, as my daughter said, was a place of "rabbits talking"); a sense of community, where grown-ups and authority figures hugged them, taught them, and gently reminded them of their manners, while their peers conspired with them in dancing, eating, and unstoppable running around.

Our family in China, during the High Holy Days. (above and center)

Chloe and Miranda with 'Rabbi' Teddy. (bottom)

As they have grown older, our daughters' appreciation of Jewish traditions grew in both breadth and depth. They have gradually learned that many of the things they came to treasure at Friday night services could also be experienced during an occasional Shabbat at home or in the homes of friends. They also came to know and love the excitement of erecting a sukkah each year and the sense, each week, of our family renewing our commitments to each other as we exchange hugs and good wishes for the week to come after Havdalah. And, in the past year, my older daughter has learned something of the limits of human understanding as I've begun to share with her that some Torah portions present us with a puzzle of meaning even as others provide us with the moral guidelines that have endured for centuries.

Fortunately for our daughters, the reality that they are both Jewish and Chinese has never seemed to them a limitation or even an "exception." Rather, at least at this stage, the challenge for our family will be for my husband and myself to do some justice to the miracle that our daughters are heirs to two magnificent traditions. In this regard, we feel truly blessed to live in a community where there are endless possibilities for friendship, education, and dissolving barriers to understanding. Our daughters attend a Mandarin language class (and have previously taken Spanish) and have learned, from their own friends, how to say, "hello" in some five other languages. It's my greatest hope that our children will continue to learn from each other – and that we will have the humility to learn from them.

the rochmes/davis family

Chapter Three   Outreach   **149**

reflections on jewish and chinese identity

by helen smolev

I am a Jew-by-choice. It all started at this place, where all of us are gathering this evening. Exactly eight years ago, with my husband and then fiancé Barry by my side, Rabbi Harold Schulweis as my converting Rabbi, I was converted to Judaism right here at American Jewish University. This is a very special place - my birth place of Judaism.

Having grown up in Communist China where no religions were allowed to be practiced at the time, I did not hesitate about learning a new religion called Judaism when Barry first asked me if I would be interested in learning about it. Barry was raised as a New York City political Jew, who always likes to be intellectually challenged. Therefore, he happily agreed to "one stone two birds" when he made a promise to me that he would study Judaism with me as I requested. And he did. So here we were, the two of us sitting in the AJU classroom. Often times, when our instructor Rabbi Neal Weinberg was teaching, I looked at Barry with my eyes and mouth wide open, very confused and said to him: "No - this is not Judaism! This is Buddhism! This is Chinese!" We both were amazed by the two oldest, richest cultures and traditions, and the values and wisdoms of life that the two share. We have called ourselves "Bu-Jews" ever since. Even though many of our discussions after class included some of the most challenging questions that leave us with unknown answers still today, one thing was quite clear – I was comfortable and connected to Judaism instantly.

I was born and raised in Shanghai, China, precisely in Hongkou district – one of the ten inner city districts of Shanghai. That was not special to me and had no meaning until one day when Barry and I saw a fascinating documentary film, "Shanghai Ghetto." In 1939, thousands of Jewish refugees escaped Nazi persecution to the only place that did not require entrance visas, i.e. Shanghai. It was in the Hongkou district. The film tells the little known story of the Jewish refugees, their relationships with the local Chinese and with the occupying Japanese army and the rich cultural life they had constructed under great hardship. It all occurred right in my childhood neighborhood! A one hundred year old high school (it used to be a Catholic school), where both my mother and sister attended school, was the school for the children of the Jewish refugees.

Sarina and Siji Smolev dress up for the Chinese New Year (above) Helen, Siji, Sarina, and Barry Smolev at an ECC Shabbat.

the smolev family

reflections on jewish and chinese identity continued

I was stunned to see how the Chinese and the Jews were living side-by-side, helping each other and surviving under the Japanese occupation. The Jews were comforted by the familiar Shanghai street food that I am still craving for from time to time. In the movie a sign says that the Jews and the Chinese needed a special permit to cross the Waibaidu Bridge (Garden Bridge). It reminded me of a sign that stated "Chinese and Dogs Are Not Allowed" in front of the entrance to the park next to the bridge. I felt a great connection to the Jewish people from that moment on and understood the true meaning of "Your People, My People."

Barry and I fell in love at first sight. We quickly and strongly connected to each other with our similar views of life and the world. Barry, like many Jews, is very comfortable with speaking up and showing his emotions. I am like most Chinese who are quiet and more reserved, especially in a public setting. As a Chinese woman, I love food. One day I made my favor childhood food, "potato with meat." Barry told me that was his long missed food from his grandmother, a homemade specialty called Potato Pirogi. I have learned and am able to make a few Jewish dishes that were commented on, "as good as it gets," in the best Jewish deli in town. I am very proud of that. Our twins, Sarina and Siji, are truly very fortunate children. They have perfectly understood right at the beginning about who they are – American Chinese Jews! They were born in the great country of America, come to the ECC at Leo Baeck Temple every day, go to a Chinese school on Saturdays and will be coming to LBT for Sunday religious school in the future. They are blessed by being the heirs to two magnificent cultures and traditions, living in this great nation of America, where everything is possible and in the diverse and welcoming LBT community where they are loved and fully belong.

As all of us are celebrating the Chinese New Year in our Leo Baeck Temple community, my wish is that someday, somewhere some important Jewish holidays will be also celebrated in a traditional Chinese community, hopefully in my children's lifetime.

Finally, I wish everyone a wonderful, healthy, prosperous New Year.

Happy Chinese New Year!

The Smolev family, Barry, Helen, and twins, Sarina and Siji on a family trip to China.

the smolev family

Chapter Three   Outreach   **151**

just for fun in the chinese new year

	Born in 1924, 1936, 1948, 1960, 1972, 1984, 1996, 2008	MICE: You are imaginative, charming, and truly generous to the person you love. However, you have a tendency to be quick-tempered and overly critical. You are also inclined to be somewhat of an opportunist. Born under this sign, you should be happy in sales or as a writer, critic, or publicist.
	Born in 1925, 1937, 1949, 1961, 1973, 1985, 1997, 2009.	BUFFALO / OX: A born leader, you inspire confidence from all around you. You are conservative methodical, and good with your hands. Guard against being chauvinistic and always demanding your own way. The Buffalo would be successful as a skilled surgeon, general, or hairdresser.
	Born in 1926, 1938, 1950, 1962, 1974, 1986, 1998, 2010.	TIGER: You are sensitive, emotional, and capable of great love. However, you have a tendency to get carried away and be stubborn about what you think is right; often seen as a "hothead" or rebel. Your sign shows you would be excellent as a boss, explorer, race car driver, or matador.
	Born in 1927, 1939, 1951, 1963, 1975, 1987, 1999, 2011.	RABBIT: You are the kind of person that people like to be around, affectionate, obliging, always pleasant. You have a tendency, though, to get too sentimental and seem superficial. Being cautious and conservative, you are successful in business but would also make a good lawyer, diplomat, or actor.
	Born in 1916, 1928, 1940, 1952, 1964, 1976, 1988, 2000, 2012.	DRAGON: Full of vitality and enthusiasm, the Dragon is a popular individual even with the reputation of being foolhardy and a "big mouth" at times. You are intelligent, gifted, and a perfectionist but these qualities make you unduly demanding on others. You would be well-suited to be an artist, priest, or politician.
	Born in 1917, 1929, 1941, 1953, 1965, 1977, 1989, 2001, 2013.	SNAKE: Rich in wisdom and charm, you are romantic and deep thinking and your intuition guides you strongly. Avoid procrastination and your stingy attitude towards money. Keep your sense of humor about life. The Snake would be most content as a teacher, philosopher, writer, psychiatrist, and fortune teller.
	Born in 1918, 1930, 1942, 1954, 1966, 1978, 1990, 2002, 2014.	HORSE: Your capacity for hard work is amazing. Your are your own person-very independent. While intelligent and friendly, you have a strong streak of selfishness and sharp cunning and should guard against being egotistical. Your sign suggests success as an adventurer, scientist, poet, or politician.
	Born in 1919, 1931, 1943, 1955, 1967, 1979, 1991, 2003, 2015.	GOAT: Except for the knack of always getting off on the wrong foot with people, the Goat can be charming company. Your are elegant and artistic but the first to complain about things. Put aside your pessimism and try to be less dependent on material comforts. You would be best as an actor, gardener, or beachcomber.
	Born in 1920, 1932, 1944, 1956, 1968, 1980, 1992, 2004, 2016.	MONKEY: You are very intelligent and have a clever wit. Because of your extraordinary nature and magnetic personality, you are always well-liked. The Monkey, however, must guard against being an opportunist and distrustful of other people. Your sign promises success in any field you try.
	Born in 1921, 1933, 1945, 1957, 1969, 1981, 1993, 2005, 2017.	ROOSTER: The Rooster is a hard worker; shrewd and definite in decision-making and often speaking his mind. Because of this, you tend to seem boastful to others. You are a dreamer, flashy dresser, and extravagant to an extreme. You should be happy as a restaurant owner, publicist, soldier, or world traveler.
	Born in 1922, 1934, 1946, 1958, 1970, 1982, 1994, 2006, 2018.	DOG: The Dog will never let you down. Born under this sign you are honest, and faithful to those you love. However, you are plagued by constant worry, a sharp tongue, and a tendency to be a fault finder. You would make an excellent businessman, activist, teacher, or secret agent.
	Born in 1923, 1935, 1947, 1959, 1971, 1983, 1995, 2007, 2019.	PIG: You are a splendid companion, an intellectual with a very strong need to set difficult goals and carry them out. You are sincere, tolerant, and honest but by expecting the same from others, you are incredibly naive. Your quest for material goods could be your downfall. The Pig would be best in the arts as an entertainer, or possible a lawyer.

resources for further learning

CHINESE NEW YEAR TRADITIONS

- **chinapage.com/newyear**
An overview.

- **educ.uvic.ca/faculty/mroth/438/CHINA/chinese_new_year.html**
In-depth exploration, with several links.

enchantedlearning.com/crafts/chinesenewyear/
A resource for children's activities pertaining to Chinese New Year

JEWISH IDENTITY ISSUES; JEWISH-CHINESE FAMILIES

- **urj.org/outreach/interfaith**
Information and resources for interfaith families from the Union for Reform Judaism.

- **thejewishmuseum.org/site/pages/onlinex.php?id=28**
Website for the Jewish Identity Project, a photographic exploration of the multiple cultural, social, racial, and ethnic faces of Jewish identity in contemporary America.

- **interfaithfamily.com/relationships/interracial_and_intercultural_relationships/How_We_Raise_Children_in_Our_Chinese-Jewish_Family.shtml**
Perspectives on raising Jewish-Chinese families.

- **nytimes.com/2007/03/08/nyregion/08batmitzvah.html?_r=1&oref=slogin**
Profile of a Chinese-Jewish adoptee becoming a bat mitzvah.

CHINESE ORPHANS AND ADOPTEES

- **fwcc.org**
Website of Families With Children from China, with extensive resources.

- **halfthesky.org**
Website of Half the Sky Foundation, nonprofit organization providing early education, nurturing, and caregiver assistance to children living in Chinese orphanages; recipient of four-star rating from Charity Navigator.

HISTORY OF THE JEWS IN CHINA

- **haruth.com/AsiaJewsShanghai**
Information, with links to multiple other websites, on the history of the Jewish communities at Shanghai

- **jewishvirtuallibrary.org/jsource/vjw/chinajews.html**
A virtual tour of Jewish history in China.

- **sino-judaic.org**
Website of the Sino-Judaic institute, including information on the Jews of Kaifeng and multiple links to sites exploring Asian jewry.

- *Bridge Across Broken Time: Chinese and Jewish Cultural Memory* by Vera Schwarcz (1998, Yale University Press)

- *The Survival of the Chinese Jews: The Jewish Community of Kaifeng* by Donald Leslie (1972, BRILL Press)

- *The Jews of China* by Jonathan Goldstein (1999, M.E. Sharp)

Chapter Three   Outreach   **153**

happy new year

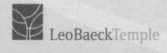

Integrating Basic Judaism Students into the Life of the Synagogue

Name of Congregation:	Congregation Beth Israel
Address:	9001 Towne Centre Drive, San Diego, CA 92122
Phone number:	(858) 535-1111
Contact's E-mail:	Bonnie Graff, bgraff@cbisd.org
Number of Member Units:	1250
URJ District:	West District
Rabbi:	Rabbi Michael Berk
Staff:	Executive Director Lesley Mills
	Program Director Bonnie Graff
	Membership & Caring Community Coordinator Lianne Gordon
Outreach Chair:	Karen Shein Christiansen
Membership Chair:	Cynthia Fram

Brief Description: Like many synagogues, we offer an Introduction to Judaism course (we call it Basic Judaism), for newcomers to Judaism. This year we took additional steps to integrate these students into the life of our synagogue in ways that encouraged continued involvement, conversion, and membership after the course was over.

Program Goal: To have Basic Judaism students feel completely comfortable, familiar, and welcomed into the life of our synagogue so that they may choose to continue their connection with us through conversion, membership, additional education, worship, or other avenues of synagogue involvement.

Target Population: Basic Judaism students who are generally newcomers to Judaism, or those seeking a refresher who wish to deepen their knowledge and appreciation of Judaism, its fundamental concepts and practice, and learn how to participate in worship and ritual life. These are individuals who may be considering or working toward conversion or who are interfaith couples wishing to be married by our clergy.

Number of Participants: Fifty.

Number and Length of Sessions: Eighteen class sessions, plus additional personal involvement as desired by the individual students.

Staffing Required: Rabbi Lenore Bohm, a well-respected area rabbi with long-time connections to our synagogue, taught the class. Two Outreach Committee members acted as liaisons and assisted in various ways. Hands-on and participatory Outreach classes that were integrated into the Basic Judaism curriculum were taught by our cantor, senior rabbi, and director of education emeritus. Our program director works with our Outreach Committee to plan the hands-on, participatory classes, and between two and six Outreach Committee members act as greeters and assist with these programs as needed. Our facilities coordinator and custodial staff help with room setup.

Total Cost of Program: Basic Judaism books, instruction, and the Outreach Shabbat dinner at the end of the course ran about $250 per person. Our hands-on participatory Outreach programs cost approximately $500 for staffing and materials.

Source of Funding: Basic Judaism students pay for the books and materials for the course and the Outreach Shabbat dinner at the end of the course. Our synagogue budget seeds the Outreach Fund for this purpose, and the Adult Learners Network Fund is available to help cover the cost of putting on our hands-on participatory programs, with Outreach members often donating some needed items and food.

Fees for Attendees: Basic Judaism students paid $200 per member, $250 per nonmember to cover the cost of books, instruction, and the Outreach Shabbat dinner. Our hands-on, participatory Outreach classes are free. The WBI Cook-Off was a minifundraiser and cost $20 per person to attend. There is no charge to participate in our mentor program.

Logistics: Our program director and Outreach Committee event chairs work with our synagogue facilities coordinator to arrange the setup of each class and event. The Basic Judaism classes took place weekly in our social hall. Seating was arranged in a U to facilitate interaction. The instructor had a table and whiteboard for her use. A refreshment table with coffee, tea, and water was set up in the room before each class, with space available for the snacks brought in each week by class members. A table with flyers, brochures, and other temple information was also available at each class. Setup for the hands-on and participatory Outreach programs varied by need, but generally also included the refreshment table, gift-shop display table, brochure/flyer table and a check-in table. Our Chanukah and Passover programs included cooking and other demonstrations, and tables near outlets were provided for them.

Instructions to Facilitator: The key to integrating the Basic Judaism students into the life of our synagogue was to encourage social interaction, first between class members, and then between class members and clergy, staff, and members of our synagogue. The rabbi, other teachers, and Outreach Committee liaisons created a warm, welcoming atmosphere both in the class and the hands-on participatory Outreach programs. Additionally there were Outreach members who were greeters at each Outreach program. Every class and program included a break for refreshments and schmoozing. Several programs offered activities such as making chanukiyot, participation in a mock seder and a Havdalah ceremony, so that students were engaged with others. Clergy made it clear that they were approachable and accessible to speak with and meet with class members.

Evaluation of Program: We send out an e-survey to participants after each Outreach program. In this way we can determine if the program met our goals and satisfied the needs of the students. The results are reviewed by the Outreach Committee, as well as by the clergy and staff involved. Through these surveys, comments made by students, and the overwhelming enthusiasm of the students to continue their involvement at our synagogue, we considered our integration strategies to be a great success.

Follow-up: We created an e-blast list of the Basic Judaism students and send them notices of upcoming events of possible interest. We paired interested students with families and a *chavurah* so that they could attend Passover seders. Our senior rabbi spoke to them at the last class to invite them to contact him for any reason, including conversion. Many of the students are already regularly attending worship services with us and have new friends who are members.

Several students going through conversion have been paired with members who will mentor them. Mentors are members who have, in most cases, undergone conversions themselves, and can become close friends as they help a newcomer to assimilate into the congregation, to feel welcomed, and to meet others. Our Mentor program has proven very successful in integrating those new to Judaism into the life of our synagogue. The students are given High Holy Days tickets. They are invited to sign up to receive our monthly *Tidings* newsletter and our weekly e-newsletter. Those completing conversion receive a year's synagogue membership free and may (with their permission) have their names published in our monthly newsletter in the Our Synagogue Family section, offering the community's congratulations. Those who become members and wish to become more involved are often invited to serve on the Outreach Committee.

Integrating Basic Judaism Students with our Clergy, Staff, and Jewish Life

Our Basic Judaism eighteen-week class is open to the community and is a prerequisite for interfaith couples being married by our clergy and for those working with our clergy toward conversion. This year we integrated our hands-on participatory Outreach classes into the curriculum so that these events were part of the class. Our hands-on classes "Light Up Your Chanukah," "Shabbat and Havdalah 101," and "Passover Step-by-Step," gave Basic Judaism students the opportunity to experience firsthand the traditions associated with these holidays, making it easier for them to incorporate these traditions into their lives. Since these classes were taught by our senior rabbi, cantor, and director of education emeritus, the Basic Judaism students had the opportunity to meet them. A social/snack time was built into each class so students could mix with the teaching clergy/staff and with others attending the event. Related holiday items from our gift shop were on display at each class so students could see the resources available for them.

Basic Judaism Liaisons Facilitate Connections

Two members of our Outreach Committee who were taking the class as a refresher served as liaisons to the class. They assisted the teaching rabbi by taking attendance and making announcements about upcoming synagogue events and services. They arranged a rotating snack schedule among class members, made phone calls to remind students when it was their week to bring the snack, helped students to connect with clergy, staff, and members to address various needs, such as the desire to attend a Passover seder at a member's home. These liaisons were also familiar faces at worship services and synagogue events to greet these students, make them feel welcome, and introduce them to others.

Mixing Newcomers and Veterans

Our "High Holy Days: Prepare to be Awed" class was designed to encourage both High Holy Day first-timers and veterans to fully appreciate the holidays and maximize their potential in their lives. Our hope that an integrated class of newcomers, existing, and even long-time members would work well in offering interesting information and inspiration to all, regardless of experience, was realized, as all survey responses gave rave reviews. A social time built into the event encouraged mixing and the forging of ties between Basic Judaism students and members.

Later in the programming year, we offered "Synagogue Geography," in which our senior rabbi took participants on a tour of our campus. This tour included basic information about ritual items and fascinating and little-known facts about the design and architecture of our seven-year-old campus and allowed for more social connecting as well. The group was a good mix of Basic Judaism students, other newcomers, and existing members. Our survey results, again, were excellent. This class also gave Basic Judaism students a chance to get to know our senior rabbi.

Still later in the year, the Basic Judaism class was encouraged to attend and participate in an all-campus Cook-Off sponsored by our Women of Beth Israel. For this event, each group, committee, chavurah, etc. was invited to submit a dish to be judged by a panel and by the attendees. This event was deliberately designed as a mixer, bringing together individuals from every group and committee at our synagogue, and the Basic Judaism class was invited as a sign of their acceptance as part of our synagogue community. This event was completely optional for Basic Judaism students, but by this time in the year, the class was a tight-knit group and comfortable mixing with our congregation. The class was well represented at this event and had a wonderful time. They became acquainted with many synagogue members and saw themselves as part our synagogue community.

158   The Outreach and Membership Idea Book Volume III

Special Recognition of the Basic Judaism Class

The end of the Basic Judaism class is marked by our Basic Judaism and Outreach Shabbat Dinner and Service. The dinner is a kind of graduation, attended by clergy, with certificates of completion and information on "next step" options of synagogue involvement presented, including the senior rabbi's invitation to call him or meet with him regarding questions about Judaism and about conversion. The service is focused on Outreach, celebrating those new to Judaism, those non-Jewish family members who help raise Jewish children, etc. Three individuals with a personal outreach or conversion story to share present short sermonettes that prove very moving to both the Basic Judaism students, who see themselves in the stories, and Jews by birth, who may not realize what individuals who choose Judaism go through. This year our sermonette presenters included one of our Basic Judaism class liaisons. Our senior rabbi also shared a story about the recent intermarriage in his own immediate family.

Shabbat and Havdallah 101
Tuesday, January 20, 7:00 p.m.
Instructor: Cantor Arlene Bernstein
Sponsored by the CBI Outreach Committee
No fee

This program, led by Cantor Arlene Bernstein, will share the blessings, rituals, food, music and other creative ideas for a joyous Shabbat in your home.

RSVP online by Tuesday, January 13 at www.cbisd.org/rsvp. For more information contact Program Director Bonnie Graff at bgraff@cbisd.org or call 858 535-1111, ext. 3800.

For more information on all our programs go to: www.cbisd.org

**Congregation Beth Israel
Outreach Committee**

WHERE — Congregation Beth Israel
9001 Towne Centre Drive
San Diego, CA 92122

Outreach Shabbat Dinner And Service

You are cordially invited to join us for this special dinner and service honoring our Basic Judaism "graduates."

TIME — 6:00 PM

DATE — Friday, March 27

RSVP — This is a catered Shabbat dinner, so RSVPs are a must.
No fee for Basic Judaism students
$25 for Adults; $9 for children (2-12)
RSVP online at www.cbisd.org/rsvp
Or mail a check to the address above

For more information or questions, contact Program Director Bonnie Graff at 858-535-1111 or bgraff@cbisd.org

Survey : Questions

Basic Judaism 2009 Survey

✻ Required Question(s)

Your response to this survey helps us plan classes and programs that best meet the needs of our community. Please take a few moments to give us your feedback.

✻ 1. Please rate this course in terms of excellence based on the criteria below

	Poor	Fair	Average	Good	Excellent
The course was accurately described	○	○	○	○	○
Rabbi Bohm demonstrated knowledge of the subject	○	○	○	○	○
Rabbi Bohm was able to convey the information	○	○	○	○	○
There was active class participation	○	○	○	○	○

✻ 2. How likely would you be to take another course from Rabbi Bohm?

I will not	Not likely	Possibly	Likely	Very Likely
○	○	○	○	○

✻ 3. How likely would you be to recommend this course to others?

I will not	Not likely	Possibly	Likely	Very likely
○	○	○	○	○

✻ 4. How did you first hear about this course?
- ☐ CBI Brochure
- ☐ CBI Flyer
- ☐ CBI Website (www.cbisd.org)
- ☐ CBI Newsletter (Tidings)
- ☐ CBI Shabbat Bulletin
- ☐ CBI Shalom Table
- ☐ CBI Weekly E-Blast

Survey : Questions   http://survey.constantcontact.com/survey/a07e2hoj3kxfsp0f9rr/_tmp/questions

☐ Email

☐ Community Website (please specify in the "other" option)

☐ Community Newspaper (please specify in the "other" option)

☐ A friend

☐ Other [_____]

5. How does this course compare to others you've taken at CBI?

350 character(s) left.

✳ 6. What did you like MOST about this course?

1,000 character(s) left.

✳ 7. What did you like LEAST about this course?

Survey : Questions

http://survey.constantcontact.com/survey/a07e2hoj3kxfsp0f9rr/_tmp/questions

1,000 character(s) left.

8. **What other courses or programs would you be interested in participating in at CBI?**

350 character(s) left.

9. **What is the best time for you to participate in a CBI course? Please check all that apply.**

☐ Weekday mornings

☐ Weekday afternoons

☐ Weekday evenings

☐ Saturdays

☐ Sundays

Comment:

500 character(s) left.

10. Feel free to provide any additional feedback here.

1,000 character(s) left.

Finish

Synagogue Geography

Brief description: Our senior rabbi took attendees on an engaging, behind-the-scenes tour that revealed little-known facts about our campus and took the mystery out of the ritual items found in the sanctuary. Newcomers to Judaism, as well as long-time members, were equally fascinated to learn details about the design of our campus, our history, and the story behind our ritual items. A glossary of terms is printed and distributed to all attendees to help them become familiar with the Hebrew words that are associated with our ritual objects as well as our customs and traditions. Afterward they enjoyed refreshments and connected with each other and had a chance to "schmooze" with the senior rabbi.

Program goal: To provide a tour of our campus that educates both the newcomer and long-time members and gives them a chance to meet each other. Additionally, to provide an opportunity for attendees to spend some time with and get to know our senior rabbi.

Target population: We saw this program as a rare opportunity to integrate newcomers to Judaism and our synagogue, and members – including long-time members – in one event. Basic Judaism students, Jewish and non-Jewish community members interested in learning more about Judaism and about our synagogue joined with members of our synagogue interested in learning more about the design of our campus, our history and stories behind our ritual items.

Number of participants: Fifty-five.

Number and length of sessions: One session on a weekday evening, from 7:00 to 9:00 p.m.

Staffing required: Custodial staff to set up refreshment table, 2-3 Outreach Committee members to donate and bring in cookies, and other treats for the social time. The senior rabbi led the tour.

Total cost of program: Negligible.

Source of Funding: Temple budget for beverage and table set up.

Fees for Attendees: Free.

Logistics: This program was promoted through announcements in the Basic Judaism class (Synagogue Geography was actually part of their course curriculum), in our temple newsletter, enewsletters, web site, flyers distributed at temple events and in Jewish community publications and web sites. Approximately 45 Basic Judaism students attended, plus 7 temple members and 4 unaffiliated community members.

The senior rabbi welcomed attendees in the sanctuary. He began his tour of our campus with a surprise – he took the group outside to the base of our entry staircase. This was very meaningful as he explained how the staircase tapers from bottom to top to gather the people together as they enter the gates. Rabbi Berk then led the group up those stairs, gathering them together as they entered through the gates and into our Jerusalem-themed courtyard. He took attendees through our Biblical garden and discussed the campus landscaping that includes trees and plants native to Israel. Throughout the tour he offered architectural and historical information in relation to Judaic traditions, values and texts.

The tour continued with the group entering the sanctuary building, where Rabbi Berk explained the history of our synagogue. He led attendees up on the Bima for a close look at the Ark and explained the origin of our different Torah scrolls and explained the Torah covers, yad, crown, and other parts of the Torah dressing. He then undressed and opened the Torah so those in attendance could get a very close and personal view. The traditions surrounding the writing of a Torah were explained, the group entered the social hall to enjoy a casual time of socializing with each other and with the rabbi while sampling refreshments brought by the Outreach Committee. A third table contained brochures and flyers featuring upcoming events and programs at the synagogue.

Instructions to facilitator: Although we had one clergy member lead the tour, we considered breaking up into two groups led by our rabbi and cantor, due to the size of the group. For a large group a megaphone is useful during the outdoor portion of the tour. Rabbi Berk asked for and answered questions throughout the tour. Each synagogue will have its own features, of course, but the information on the architectural and historical significance of the synagogue structures, grounds and the synagogue history are of particular interest to members and long-time members. The information about ritual items and the intimate view of the Ark, Torah and other ritual items is especially powerful for newcomers to Judaism. Rabbi Berk and our Outreach Committee members in attendance seized upon the opportunity to introduce newcomers to members and long-time members during the social time so that connections could be made.

Evaluation of program: We send out an e-survey (created with Constant Contact) to participants after each Outreach program. In this way we determine if the program met our goals and satisfied the needs of the students. The results are reviewed by the Outreach Committee, as well as by the clergy and staff involved. Responses to this event were very favorable and enthusiastic. In addition, the Outreach Committee members who attended critiqued the event and made notes indicating what we could do to improve it next year.

Follow-up: The attendance list was used to supplement our e-mailing list so that all attendees receive notices of future events. Our clergy also encouraged attendees to contact them with any questions.

Chapter Three   Outreach   **167**

Tashlikh And Self-Improvement

Suggestions from Rabbi Allen S. Maller
(With a few changes from Rabbi Bohm)

My Sins	*Midot: My Opportunities*
What I positively **do not** want to be:	What I positively **do** want to be:
Angry	Peaceful/content
Judgmental	Accepting
Stubborn	Open-minded
A perfectionist	Flexible
Uncertain	Willing
Jealous	Grateful
Cynical	Appreciative
Materialistic	Charitable
Fearful	Confident
Self-deprecating	Self Respecting
Irresponsible	Attentive; a mitzvah-doer
Hostile	Supportive
Defensive	Open to advice & guidance

## Self-Awareness exercise for Yom Kippur

from "You Shall be Holy: A Code of Jewish Ethics"
by Rabbi Joseph Telushkin

Am I prone to anger? When I am angry, do I overreact and sayar do things that inflict pain on others? Or am I the sort of person wbo, if asked, will deny that I am angry yet will treat other people with coldness, disdain and annoyance?

Do I judge others fairly, or am I harshly critical, both in what I say and what I think?

Am I stingy with my money or my time?

Do I speak curtly, making people feel that I have no time for them?

Do I avoid saying or doing what I believe is right because I fear how others will react or what they will think of me?

Am I moody? Do I make people around me feel that they are somehow responsible for my moods? Does my unhappiness affect the atmosphere in my home, transforming, aften in a matter of minutes, a general feeling of pleasantness and goodwill inta one of tension and sadness?

Do I treat strangers with more consideration than members of my own family?

Do I take other people's kind behavior for granted, or do I go out of my way to express thanks and help those who have been kind to me?

Do I blame my wrongful actions and mistakes on others, or do I take responsibility for the wrong I do?

Do I jump to conclusions and blame other people before I know all the facts?

Am I able to control my impulses or do I give in to temptation easily?

Do I bear grudges and remain angry at others for a long time after an argument?

Am I tardy and thereby waste other people's time by keeping them waiting?

Do I rationalize dishonesty with excuses such as "Business is different?"

When I hear of other people's sufferings or misfortunes, do I find ways to help them, or do I feel sadness in my heart but do nothing?

Am I jealous of the success of others? Do I begrudge others their good fortune?

Six Common "Weaknesses" to Avoid

1. Insatiability – the desire for more

2. Rationalization – makes repentance and self-improvement impossible

3. Having a greater concern with prevailing in an argument than with being right –perverse desire to dispute any assertion made by those we regard as opponents

4. Letting pride or stubbornness stop me from acknowledging a mistake

5. Wasting time – consider: "I have plenty of time" means there is something empty or missing in our life. "I have no time at all" becomes a rationale for not doing things we can do.

6. Being indifferent to someone else's suffering

Sermonette for Outreach Shabbat '09

by Hannah Leavenworth

Getting a first impression of me you might first notice the Star of David around my neck and my tendencies to say "sorry I have to be at temple that day,"and think, "she's a nice Jewish girl." But what you wouldn't realize is that I am what my friend has affectionately termed a hybrid. Both of my parents come from very different religious backgrounds and believe very different things, yet here I am standing in this temple today.

My mother comes from a small town in Pennsylvania where you are bound to meet at least one Frank, or Levitz related to me. Her family was very religious and she was brought up in a strong Jewish community. As she grew up and moved away she became less involved. It was not an intentional choice, but just a side effect of college and her busy life. When she met and married my dad my Popup was supportive of her non-Jewish mate. Unfortunately we will never know what my Mumum would have thought of him.

After getting married they made the best choice of their lives. They had me. They had no immediate plans to bring me up in any religion until Christmas time when I was 4 years old. Walking around looking at Christmas lights we passed a house with a manger scene and I proudly pointed and said, "Look mom it's baby Jesus." My preschool teacher had read us the story that day and I was excited to show what I had learned. Something in my mother snapped to attention and she turned to my father and said, " She's going to the JCC." So off to the JCC preschool I went. Soon we joined CBI and I began in the religious school here, joined the choir and enjoyed the time I spent at temple.

Now before I go on I think it is important to explain my father. He is the most Jewish non-Jew you will ever meet. At least now he is. He grew up here in California in a semi-Christian home. They occasionally visited church, but no one in the family was really into it.. He and his parents have always been amazingly supportive of me in my religion. He knows all the holidays, comes to services with us, and, in my opinion, makes the best latkes in the world. My grandparents are great too, because every year when a holiday comes up they have me explain it, because they want to understand and be supportive of that part of my life. My grandma even wanted to come to Yom Kippur services to hear me chant this year.

That leads me to well, me. Like all young Jewish kids at the age of thirteen I had my Bat Mitzvah. I remember at my last bat mitzvah rehearsal the Cantor cried and said how amazing it was that my dad was so supportive of all that I had done. Afterwards my mom told me that I would have to attend our CBI high school for a year and then after that it was up to me. My close friends from years past had left the temple and I was not all that keen on going back without them. I will always be thankful that she made me go that year because that was when I really got to know the awesome woman that is the Cantor. I chose teen choir as my elective and that is where I made some of my best friends at this temple. Then I discovered BITY, the temple youth group, went on to Confirmation and made many more friends.

That is when we took the trip to DC. I had never felt so close to my classmates, religion, and culture before. We had services every day, and as a group100 reform Jewish teens we held havdala on the steps of the Jefferson memorial. We learned about Jewish views on world events and stayed up on way too much caffeine writing our speeches for lobbying the next day. But the most amazing moment to me took place the day we visited the holocaust museum. As we one by one finished the exhibit and met in the large stone room at the end of the museum, we gathered in a circle and held hands. We recited the words of the mourners Kaddish, and as our voices echoed through the room, I felt so close to the people that had died and so strongly connected to Judaism.

That brings me to this past year. Cantor mentioned that she wanted to take a trip to Israel with the choir. My mother and were very excited about it, but my dad was unsure, feeling he would be out of place as a non-Jew. After persuasion by my mother, me and the Cantor, plus a little of that old Jewish guilt tripping, he agreed to come. On that trip my father, along with the rest of my family, gained a new family and had an amazing time. The people we were with embraced my dad for the great guy that he is. And now he has a group of Jewish dads to play backgammon with. He feels accepted here, which is the best part about this temple. Although the whole trip was wonderful the highlight came from simply being wished Shabbat shalom by a stranger on the street, something so mundane, yet something I know wouldn't happen any other place but in Israel.

Through all my experiences I have helped my mom rediscover her religion, helped my dad find some nice Jewish friends, and most importantly have a culture and a religion I feel strongly about. I may not be part of a conventional family, but who wants to be anyway? I love being the hybrid I am. The uniqueness within this temple, within the reform movement, is what makes us special. All of us different ages, from different backgrounds, and for different reasons are brought together through this religion and are given a place like home to feel safe.

Sermonette for Outreach Shabbat '09

by Linda Vuong

What does a Jew look like? Somebody with curly hair, brown eyes and fair skin? Well, whatever your answer, it probably isn't somebody who looks like me. Since I know people look at me and wonder "What's her story?" I've decided to be very open about my conversion. Why not explain? And I've gotten an amazing response because of my transparency. I have found Beth Israel to be a completely warm, welcoming and supportive place.

So here's my story. My parents were Vietnamese refugees. And although I was born in the States, I was raised with a strong cultural awareness of Vietnam. I first became aware of Judaism in 6th grade. That year everybody in our class was invited to Andrew Berg's bar mitzvah. There was a big party and food and a DJ, but what I remember most clearly was Andrew's beautiful Torah reading. I was so intrigued that I had to learn more – and the more I learned, the more surprised I was by how connected I felt to Judaism.

What struck me first was the emphasis placed on the importance of family. Coming from an Asian background, I instantly related to this value – one that I think is often missing in the greater American society. It's been said that more than the Jewish people have kept Shabbat, Shabbat has kept the Jewish people. But what makes Shabbat the joyful holiday that it is, is family. Lighting candles together, blessing the children, stopping once a week to enjoy a beautiful meal together. It is *family* that has kept the Jewish people all these millennia.

As I grew older and learned more about Judaism, I was able to value it on an intellectual level. I took a humanities course on the Torah, I came to understand that Judaism encourages learning, challenging and questioning. After all, "Israel" literally means "to struggle with God." Here was a religion that recognizes people can and do have a difficult time finding God and balancing past traditions with modern life, and it's okay not to know all the answers. How refreshing.

Also, I love Judaism's passion for social justice. One of my coworkers who is gay was delighted when he found out I'm Jewish. He and his partner have been intrigued by Judaism but too afraid to approach a rabbi for fear of rejection. I was so proud to tell him that not only had my congregation married same sex couples, but we've even married *interfaith* same sex couples!

At the heart of my love for Judaism is its enduring relevancy to my life. I've come a long way from that 13-year-old girl who was so moved at Andrew Berg's bar mitzvah, but Judaism's teachings continue to offer me much to rejoice in and struggle with.

What I hope to give back to Judaism and to this congregation is to raise awareness about how the face of Judaism is changing. I learned last year when Rabbi Berk's brother addressed the congregation that there's actually a thriving Vietnamese community in Tel Aviv. Since I hope to go on a Birthright trip to Israel next year, I'm looking forward to trying all the fantastic Vietnamese restaurants I've heard about!

I've also learned about Chinese girls being raised by Jewish families in America. In response to China's one child policy, and a preference for sons, many Chinese couples abandon their daughters. As many as 55,000 of these girls are being raised by North Americans, many of them Jewish. So these girls are growing up as Jewish as Andrew Berg – they're even starting to have their own b'not mitzvah. So maybe someday when somebody asks you what a Jew looks like, you'll think of straight dark hair, olive complexions and almond shaped eyes.

You are a Basic Judaism Graduate....

So now what??

We would like to first congratulate you on your successful completion of the class. It is a big commitment, yet the reward is immeasurable.

Now that you may not come to CBI every Tuesday evening, we want to tell you about all there is still to participate in. Remember, most events and activities are open to non-members, including services, yet we would be amiss if we did not mention that members are the heart of our synagogue and we would be lucky to have you as a member.

First, our High Holy Days are celebrated at the Civic Center. Tickets are necessary and are included as part of becoming a member. As a BJ graduate, you each get a free ticket to the High Holy Days too!

So the following are some ways to stay involved:

1. www.cbisd.org We have an award winning website that is chock full of information.

2. The Tidings Newsletter is available in print or on the website. It is published monthly and edited by our very own Outreach Committee chairperson, Karen Shein. Read the online (clickable from the home page) or call Heather at 858 535-1111, ext. 3126 to be added to the mailing list. Members automatically receive Tidings.

3. CBI E-newsletters go out weekly and provide you with the latest on events, activities and services at CBI. Sign up on the Web site.

4. Join a chavarah. Each Chavurah is a small group of Temple members who come together to learn, to socialize and to enjoy Jewish living with their families. They study together, worship together, celebrate Jewish holidays together, eat together. For many, the Chavurah is an extended family. See the website for more information.

5. Come to the numerous programs and classes offered. The schedule of events is always on the Web site and in Tidings.

Only you know why you really participated in the BJ class. There are many reasons to take the class, from just the joy of learning to conversion. No matter your reason, we want to help you move to the next step. If you just want to stay involved with the synagogue, slowly dipping your toe into Jewish life, then the above list will help you the most.

If you want to know more about how to go the next step in your conversion or how to begin a conversation regarding a Jewish wedding:

1. Meet with Rabbi Berk or Cantor Bernstein. Contact Rabbi's assistant, Gail Malkus at gmalkus@cbisd.org, or 858 535-1111, ext. 3110, or the Cantor's assistant, Susan Hutchinson at shutchison@cbisd.org, or 858 535-1111, ext. 3116. You will find they are very accessible and you will feel at home speaking with either of them.

Chapter Three   Outreach   **175**

2. Mentorship is available for conversion candidates. When you go to the clergy to begin your journey to conversion, let them know you are interested in a mentor. Our mentors are friendly and helpful CBI members who understand what it's like to be new to Judaism and to CBI and often become good friends.

On behalf of the clergy and the Outreach Committee, we again congratulate you on your accomplishment and dedication. We hope to see you throughout your adventures at CBI and please feel free to contact us with any questions.

Contact information below:

Rabbi Berk at rabbiberk@cbisd.org, with assistant Gail Malkus at gmalkus@cbisd.org, or 858 535-1111, ext. 3110

Cantor Bernstein at abernstein@cbisd.org, with assistant Susan Hutchinson at shutchison@cbisd.org, or 858 535-1111, ext. 3116

Bonnie Graff at bgraff@cbisd.org, with assistant Matt Cromwell at mcromwell@cbisd.org or 858-535-1111, ext 3112

Netanya Dayzie at netanya@cybercranny.com, with no assistant, or 760-420-2994

176 The Outreach and Membership Idea Book Volume III

Light Up Your Chanukah

Tuesday, December 16
7:00 p.m.

Experience Chanukah, one of the most joyful celebrations of Judaism, in this fun-filled, hands-on workshop. You'll learn how to cook traditional foods, make your own menorah and learn about Chanukah rituals and history.

Presented by Director of Education Emeritus Helene Schlafman and the Outreach Committee.

No fee. For planning purposes please RSVP by Friday, Dec. 12 at
WWW.CBISD.ORG/RSVP
For questions, contact Program Director Bonnie Graff at 858-535-1111 ext. 3800 or bgraff@cbisd.org

For more information on all our CBI programs go to: www.cbisd.org/outreach

The High Holy Days: Prepare to be Awed!

Tuesday September 23
7:00 – 9:00 p.m.
with Rabbi Lenore Bohm
Feuerstein Family Activity Center

A class designed to encourage both High Holy Day first-timers and veterans to fully appreciate this incredible season of reflection and renewal. Topics to be discussed:

* Major Rosh Hashanah and Yom Kippur themes and highlights of seasonal customs and rituals
* The traditional spiritual message of the Holy Days
* Creative ideas on how to maximize their potential in your life

RSVP online at www.cbisd.org/rsvp. For more information or to RSVP, contact Program Director Bonnie Graff at 858-535-1111 ext. 3800 or email bgraff@cbisd.org.

Synagogue Geography

Tuesday, February 17 7:00 p.m.
Location: Glickman-Galinson Sanctuary

Rabbi Michael Berk takes you on a fascinating, behind-the scenes tour that reveals little-known facts about our campus and takes the mystery out of the ritual items found in the sanctuary. Afterwards you'll enjoy refreshments as you connect with others exploring Judaism and have a chance to "shmooze" (socialize) with Rabbi Berk.

This program is part of the *Basic Judaism* offerings and is open to all.

There is no fee, but please RSVP for planning purposes.

RSVP online by Thursday, February 12 at www.cbisd.org/rsvp. For more information contact Program Director Bonnie Graff at bgraff@cbisd.org or call 858 535-1111, ext. 3800.

For information on this and other Outreach programs, go to www.cbisd.org

Congregation Beth Israel Outreach Committee

Jewish Children of Interfaith Families

Congregation:	Ohef Sholom Temple
Address:	530 Raleigh Avenue, Norfolk, Va 23507
Phone number:	757-625-4295
Contact's Name and E-mail:	Gary Bernstein, gary@ohefsholom.org
Number of Member Units:	670
URJ District:	South District
Rabbi:	Rosalin Mandelberg
Interfaith Committee Chairs:	Shannon Bartel, Stephanie Galbraith, Ann Konikoff

Brief Description: A panel discussion with Ohef Sholom congregants. This program featured three young adult offspring of interfaith families, all of whom were *b'nei mitzvah* and confirmed at Ohef Sholom. Each spoke about the experiences, challenges, and strengths of being raised as a Jew in an interfaith family.

Program Goals: To educate interfaith families about how to make Jewish choices in raising their children and to show all members, by example, that vibrant Jewish life can take place in interfaith homes.

Target Population: Interfaith families from Ohef Sholom and the community at large.

Number of Participants: Sixty.

Number and Length of Sessions: One session, lasting 1 hour and 30 minutes.

Staffing Required: Gary Bernstein, Director of Congregational Life, Rabbi Mandelberg.

Total Cost of Program: $50.00.

Source of Funding: Program budget.

Logistics: Sign-up sheet, name tags, survey forms, pencils, coffee, fruit, bagels, juice.

Instruction to facilitator: Have facilitator create a series of questions, in advance, for each of the panelists. Each panelist will share his or her story, with the facilitator creating an atmosphere of openness and sensitivity.

Evaluation of Program: Twenty-three out of the sixty participants took part in the program evaluation immediately following the panel discussion. Sixteen indicated that they liked hearing the panelist's stories. Fifteen liked the group discussion.

Follow-up: As a result of this well-received program, four new Interfaith programs were developed with four different thematic issues in four different locations to begin in May and run through July 2009.

Newsletter Article

If Your Mother is Christian and Your Father is Jewish, What Does That Make You?

Few topics in the Jewish community raise passionate opinions like "Interfaith Marriage." Study after study, statistic after statistic and proclamation after proclamation render a judgment and projection about the impact of this group of Jewish families on the future of the Jewish people.

Some say, only 1/3 of the children of inter-faith families are raised as Jews; they, in turn, only raise their children as Jews at the rate of 1 out of 3, and so on and so forth, so that by the third generation, there are no more people in these families who identify themselves as Jews.

Others say, inter-faith families are affected by the exact same factors as (what are called) in-faith families in terms of determining Jewish identity. If the family is Jewishly active and identified – – belonging to a synagogue, attending services and activities in the temple and Jewish community, going to Jewish summer camps and Youth Group events, traveling to Israel, having Jewish friends and being an active part of a Jewish community – all of these life choices determine a child's Jewish identity and likelihood that he or she will also raise a Jewish family regardless of whether one of his or her parents is not Jewish.

At Ohef Sholom, we don't look at our Temple Family members as statistics. We view every one who walks through our doors as a partner in our Jewish life, with something valuable to contribute with your presence alone. Our goal is always to model the most vibrant and meaningful Jewish way of life we can, so that active participation in our Jewish heritage is something you long for, look forward to, find fulfilling and that you enjoy, not some desperate effort to hold onto the last dying remnant of our people. We find that families that are engaged in their own Jewish lives and the educations of their children identify 100% as Jewish and feel good about their religious identity, period.

To that end, our **Interfaith Outreach Committee** is sponsoring a panel and discussion, entitled: **"Jewish Children of Interfaith Families: A Panel Discussion with OST Congregants."** The program will take place, **Sunday, February 15, at 10:15 a.m. in Room 310**. It will feature three of our young adult children – – Jennifer Higgins, Leigh Nusbaum and Matthew Schoner – all of whom were B'nai Mitzvah and Confirmed at our synagogue. Each will speak about his or her experience, challenges they faced and strength they gained, from being raised as Jews in inter-faith families. I know you will be moved, inspired and educated by what they have to teach us. All are welcome, including grandparents! Light refreshments will be served.

It is the hope of our Interfaith Outreach Committee and all of us at OST that not only do you come away from this program with new information, but also that you see how much we value every member of our OST community as they are, for who they are. Judaism is good enough and precious enough to be lived out and transmitted by any one who casts their lot with us and chooses to do so. Won't you join us for this wonderful morning!?! Yours truly, your moderator too, looks forward to greeting you.

Fondly,

Rabbi Roz

Facilitator Preparations for Panel

We are so looking forward to our panel on Sunday and have done much publicity and heard great interest from many people. I wanted to offer my help to any of you who might like it. I/we were hoping that you would each speak for about 10-20 minutes about:

1) what your family make up is (who is Jewish and who is another faith or no other faith) and what decisions or agreements they made about how you were going to be raised?

2) How did that work out early on? How did you navigate holidays, relatives on each side of your family? And how did they deal with your family?

3) What was your Jewish education like, both formally (in Religious School, Bar and Bat Mitzvah, Confirmation, teaching assistant and/or teacher) and informally (OSTY, BBYO, in college if applicable, or in making a choice about colleges)?

4) What were some of the challenges you faced growing up in an inter-faith household? Did you ever feel torn? Judged by family members on either side or by outsiders questioning your Judaism?

5) Were there any particular benefits? Did it make your sense of your Judaism stronger or more important?

6) How do you feel about being Jewish yourself? How strong is y our Jewish identity? Do you feel strongly about raising your own Jewish family? Is it important to you to marry someone Jewish or to have them convert or not? Would it matter if your boyfriend/girlfriend spouse actively practiced a different religion?

7) Anything else you might want to add? Or any advice you might want to give people struggling with raising their kids? Is it preferable to have one religion?

After you speak, we will take questions. I'm moderating, so I will be right there with you helping to answer these questions.

The program is called for 10:15 am and will run no later than noon.

Thank you so much for your time. Please feel free to call me or email me if you have any questions at all.

Fondly,

Rabbi Roz

Rabbi Roz Mandelberg

Ohef Sholom Temple

Ohef Sholom Temple's Interfaith Outreach Committee Presents:

4 New Programs

. . . that Welcome, Support and Engage Interfaith families by providing opportunities to meet one another and the education needed to make the most sensitive choices for your family.

All 4 sessions will be led by Rabbi Roz Mandelberg.

RSVP at least 1 week prior to the event to Gary Bernstein at gary@ohefsholom.org or 757-625-4295

Program #1:
"There's an Easter egg on your Seder plate!"

Sunday, May 31st, 2009
starting at 10:30 am at
Ohef Sholom Temple

For young interfaith couples, committed to raising Jewish children, who are addressing the challenges of holidays and life-cycle celebrations. Come meet friends and make new ones, learn from each other and feel encouraged and light brunch and babysitting will be provided.

Program #2:
"Trying to figure it all out!"

Sunday, June 7th, 2009
starting at 10:30 am at
Ohef Sholom Temple

For interfaith couples anticipating their upcoming weddings, the birth and ongoing raising of children, including B'nai Mitzvah observances, or your children's weddings. In a safe environment, share your journey with one another as you find an understanding and supportive community in which to grow as a couple and a family. A light brunch and babysitting will be provided.

Program #3:
"How are your grandkids being raised in an interfaith family?"

Wednesday, June 24th, 2009
starting at 7:30 pm, at the home of
Dolores and Alan Bartel:
7510 Oceanfront Avenue
Virginia Beach, Virginia 23451

A forum for grandparents, whose children are or will be intermarrying, to talk about what this will mean for your grandchildren's religious upbringing, how you will handle your children's decisions (what you might say or not say) and what their choices will mean for you and for the future of the Jewish people? Coffee and dessert will be provided.

Program #4:
"Oy Vey! Look who's coming to dinner!"

Tuesday, July 7th, 2009, 7:30 pm, at the home of Steve and Sally Kocen:
4521 Lodgepole Dr.
Virginia Beach, Virginia 23462

For parents to share your questions and concerns about your child's choice to date someone of another faith. Talk with other parents, and Rabbi Roz, about how to address your fears and navigate these unfamiliar waters. Coffee and dessert will be provided.

---

www.ohefsholom.org

Chapter Four

College and 20s/30s: Nurturing Connections to Our Jewish Community

It is vital to find ways to reach out to college students and maintain their connection to the Jewish community. That need for outreach continues into their twenties and thirties. The communication revolution and their sense of what makes up a Jewish community affect how and where we reach them. The following three programs effectively used technology to communicate and nurture.

Reaching college students is best done by using other college students, their professors, and technology. Temple B'nai Israel invited area Jewish college and university students via Facebook, Hillel, temple monthly bulletin, e-mail, and personal invitation to join the temple for a special *Sha'arei Shabbat* in their honor. Dinner was provided at no cost with a college ID, and the discussion group topic was Jewish Life on Today's College Campus. Students had a strong feeling of being welcomed and affiliated with a community, no matter where their lives were taking them.

Young adults in their twenties and thirties often view a Jewish community as being about more than their parents' synagogue. Temple Israel realized that twenty – and thirty-year-olds seek a variety of social and spiritual encounters. To engage this group, they offered the **Community Six-Pack**, a package of community enterprises, for a single modest expense. In order to attract a pool of prospective Community Six-Pack members, they introduced an additional program, Jews Around Memphis (JAM), a series of events designed to appeal specifically to the social and spiritual interests of young adults. The results were tremendous!

Temple Sinai wanted to provide meaningful opportunities for twenty – and thirty-somethings to explore Jewish tradition and enrich their Jewish experience. *Gesher* (**Bridge**) links young adults in their twenties and thirties to a welcoming, diverse, Reform Jewish community, even if they are not yet members of Temple Sinai. Some programs involve social action, some involve Jewish learning, some involve holiday celebrations. . . . All involve socializing and fun! The program has increased the connection between people in their twenties and thirties and Temple Sinai.

Sha'arei Shabbat

Congregation:	Temple B'nai Israel
Address:	4901 N. Pennsylvania, Oklahoma City, OK 73112
Phone number:	405-242-0965
Contact's Name and E-mail:	Joel Guskin, guskin@yahoo.com
Number of Member Units:	350
URJ District:	South District
Rabbi:	Barry Cohen
Outreach Chair:	Joel Guskin

Brief Description: *Sha'arei Shabbat* is a monthly activity incorporating an early Shabbat service, dinner (from different restaurants), and various activities for children, teens, and adults, including crafts, open gym, movie, and adult discussion. Local Jewish college and university students were invited via Facebook, Hillel, temple monthly bulletin, e-mail and personal invitation to join the temple for this special *Sha'arei Shabbat* in their honor. Dinner was provided at no cost with a college ID, and the discussion group topic was Jewish Life on Today's College Campus. Student had a strong feeling of being welcome; we provided an event that gave them the sense of being affiliated with a community no matter where their lives were taking them.

Program Goals: Extending our hands to local students to continue our temple's tradition of openness while providing college students a Jewish connection wherever their lives are taking them. Our intent was to also assist Oklahoma University's Alpha Epsilon Pi Jewish fraternity and JEWLS (Jewish Ladies) women's group by being a sponsor of their Latkes for Love fundraiser, with proceeds going to Shaare Zedek Children's Hospital. This gave us a chance to model mutual cooperation.

Target Population: Jewish college-age students living locally or at Oklahoma University.

Number of Participants: Twenty-two.

Number and Length of Sessions: Service (1 hour) followed by dinner and a 90-minute discussion group.

Staffing Required: Regular group from *Sha'arei Shabbat* (8 people) plus 4 Jewish studies college professors.

Total Cost of Program: $300 including Temple contribution for "Latkes for Love" fundraiser.

Source of Funding: Sha'arei Shabbat and Outreach Committee.

Fees for attendees: No fee for college students, Hillel director, or guest professors. There was a $7 fee for all others.

Chapter Four   College and 20s/30s   **185**

Instructions to Facilitator: Maintain topic of Jewish life on college campus, allowing for interaction and open discussion.

Evaluation of Program: Some of these students are from our own temple family. Many others had never been to our temple and welcomed the opportunity to join the evening's activities, which included a hot meal provided after services. As the program's goal was to make the students feel welcome and at home the program was successful. We expect to have even better attendance next year.

Follow-up: We had discussions with the leaders of various Jewish organizations on campus for feedback and ways to improve the event. Better coordination of transportation was the main area needing improvement.

facebook Home Profile Friends Inbox

🗓 Free Shabbat Dinner at the Temple to Raise Money for Latkes for Love!!!
The Temple will be donating towards Latkes for Love - up to $200!

Host:	Latkes for Love . . . The Committee to Save the World!!!!!
Type:	Causes - Fundraiser
Network:	Global
Date:	Friday, November 14, 2008
Time:	6:00pm - 9:00pm
Location:	Temple B'nai Israel
Street:	4901 N. Pennsylvania Ave.
City/Town:	Oklahoma City, OK
	View Map ▼
Phone:	2146930433
Email:	bethann.rubin@sbcglobal.net

Description

For every student who shows up (with their student ID) Temple B'nai Israel will donate money towards Latkes for Love up to $200!!!

6:00 Services
7:00 Taco Dinner
Oneg
8:00 Discussion about Jewish Life on Campus in Oklahoma

Please help support Latkes for Love!

****** must RSVP through this link! VERY VERY IMPORTANT*********

http://www.thetempleokc.org/community/nov._14th_dinner_reservations/

Community Six-Pack

Congregation:	Temple Israel
Address:	1376 East Massey Road, Memphis, TN
Phone number:	901-761-3130
Contact's Name and E-mail:	Rabbi Adam Grossman, Celia Mutchnick
	rabbiadam@timemphis.org; celiam@timemphis.org
Number of Member Units:	1650
URJ District:	South District
Rabbis:	Rabbi Micah Greenstein, Senior rabbi
	Rabbi Adam Grossman, Assistant rabbi
	Harry K. Danziger, Rabbi Emeritus
	Cantor John Kaplan
Membership Chair:	Judy Royal

Brief Description: We realized that twenty- and thirty-year-olds seek a variety of social and spiritual encounters because, unlike older generations, this age group (a) includes significant numbers who were exposed to little or no Judaism, (b) is accustomed to having a wide range of choices as to entertainment and other activities, and (c) seeks value for their dollars and likes a "deal." To engage this group, we offered the Community Six-Pack, a package of community enterprises for a single modest expense. In order to attract a pool of prospective Community Six-Pack members, we utilized an additional program, Jews Around Memphis (JAM), a series of events designed to appeal specifically to the social and spiritual interests of people in their twenties and thirties.

The Community Six-Pack includes a one-year membership to Temple Israel, a six-month membership to the Memphis Jewish Community Center, a one-year membership to Bravo ArtsMemphis (a cultural and social Memphis arts program), two tickets to the Memphis Symphony Orchestra, a one-year subscription to the *Hebrew Watchman* (local Jewish weekly) and a donation to the Memphis Jewish Federation. While the six included in the pack are not all Jewishly oriented, the pack conveys the message that Judaism is not an isolated phenomenon but a vital part of a diverse life with a broad range of interests. (Note: Other congregations might access different types of community organizations for similar partnering.)

A bonus included in this year's membership was an exclusive VIP reception before the Bravo ArtsMemphis opera event. This event provided new members an opportunity to meet each other in a smaller setting and Temple Israel the chance to convey our appreciation for their membership. Following this event, our Temple Israel Connections Committee contacted members personally to foster their integration in our community.

The JAM schedule of events, which follows, included three major "anchor" events that would be attractive to everyone; several smaller-scale events geared to different subsets, such as young families, singles, and couples within the group; and additional community events through our nonprofit partner, Bravo ArtsMemphis. These events especially appealed to non-Jewish partners or Jews by choice, making them feel welcome and part of the Memphis Jewish community and particularly wel-

The Outreach and Membership Idea Book Volume III

come at Temple Israel. Although JAM participants were not required to purchase the Community Six-Pack in order to attend the JAM events, a number of them joined the temple. By experiencing entertaining programs such as "A Sweet Soiree," "Dim Sum and Dreidels," and "The Art of Food—A Hands-on Shabbat Experience," as well as finding a group of new friends, they felt connected to Judaism and to Temple Israel.

While a key element of this program is to engage young adults through fun and exciting programming, it is also vital to involve these individuals in active leadership roles. Group members were given the opportunity to help design and plan the JAM group, as well as to find leadership opportunities throughout the temple, thus enabling them to develop a meaningful and long-lasting connection to Temple Israel.

Program Goals:

1. To develop a core community of young Jewish adults who will become committed to the future of the Memphis Jewish community and Temple Israel.

2. To engage young Jewish adults ranging in age from 22 to 39 in Memphis Jewish life.

3. To build and maintain a warm, inviting, active Jewish community.

4. To identify and inspire strong lay leadership to help plan, facilitate, and sustain this temple community.

Target Population: Members of the community (a) who are between the ages of 22 and 39, (b) who are Jewish, partners of Jews, or seeking to become Jewish, and (c) who have never individually been members of Temple Israel. We emphasized that participants were welcome whether single, a couple, or a family with young children.

Number of participants: About 200 individuals participated in various Jews Around Memphis events. Ten single members and ten couples/young families joined Temple Israel through this package in its inaugural year.

Staffing Required: Rabbi Adam Grossman and Youth Director Celia Mutchnick managed the Community Six-Pack program, along with the JAM events. They worked closely with the initial committee to lay the groundwork and plan for the year. Lay leaders within the program were instrumental in planning specific events, and will continue to play a greater role moving forward. While both Rabbi Grossman and Celia Mutchnick attended every event, this is a program that can be successfully conducted with minimal staff participation, if carefully planned.

Total Cost of Program: Once established, the program pays for itself, as participants cover the cost of activity fees. Communication and invitations to events were predominantly done via online avenues such as our 20s and 30s webpage (www.timemphis.org/about/jam.htm), Facebook, Evite, and e-mail, which minimized administrative costs. However, ideally in the start-up phases of this program, congregations should provide some funding—we would recommend an amount sufficient to offset event costs for participants, so as to encourage attendance.

Source of Funding: Grants from the Mildred H. and Edgar C. Haas Family Endowment for Education at Temple Israel fund, the Temple Israel WRJ-Sisterhood and MRJ-Brotherhood helped to establish a base amount for the program.

Fee for Potential Members: The cost for a Community Six-Pack was $195 for singles and $285 for couples and families. The one-year membership began September 1, 2008, and expired on August 31, 2009.

Logistics: The first step of this program was to contact various community organizations to ask them to take part in our Community Six-Pack. Next, we focused on promotion of the program, an essential part of our success. By utilizing the temple's new website, Facebook, Evite.com, flyers, Memphis media outlets, and our internal e-mail distribution list, we were connected to the community on many levels. The Web page is constantly updated with pictures, calendar, and information about the Community Six-Pack. The Web page also gives users the ability to sign up for the Community Six-Pack, be added to our e-mail distribution list, RSVP for upcoming events, and pay for events online. (Note: Included are samples of the Evite.com and e-mail invitations, flyers, a newspaper article, a picture of our Web page, and a picture of a local television station's newscast promoting our "Dreidels and Dim Sum" event.)

Our e-mail list, comprising over 200 new names, was developed in a variety of ways, including collecting information at events via raffles, services, friends of friends, and online. At the beginning of this endeavor, a "welcoming committee" was established. At events, this team of charismatic conversationalists met, learned about, and engaged individuals to help build personal relationships and communal networks. In addition, following the events, personal follow-up phone calls were made and e-mails were sent to each prospective member. Finally, to ensure maximum attendance, it was important for us to provide childcare at each event.

Evaluation of Program: Based on the results below, the program was considered a great success:

1. An increase in Temple membership in the 20s and 30s age bracket.

2. The creation of a large and growing contact information list.

3. Positive feedback from internal and external parties about program and events.

4. Identification of individuals and their interest in active leadership positions.

5. Ever-growing attendance numbers as well as a growing number of responses to events.

6. Recognition of relationships formed and sustained between members of the group.

Follow-up: Building on the first year's success, the group is committed to continue reaching out with the Community Six-Pack to "transplants" and inactive young Jews whose parents belong to Temple Israel. In order to encourage the inaugural members to gradually become full members of Temple Israel, a secondary tier of membership has been created for those initial participants. The secondary package will include an increase in the membership fee; however, participants will also be given additional exciting incentives. By building onto this program year by year, we think people will form an emotional attachment to our community and thus be willing to make the financial commitment of temple membership a priority. Organizations that have already agreed to participate in this special second-year package are the Stax Museum of Soul Music, the Dixon Gallery of Art, the Memphis Botanic Gardens, and the Memphis Redbirds.

Simultaneously, plans for innovative programming will continue to move forward. New events scheduled for next year include Jewish parenting classes for young adults, social action projects within the Memphis community, and creative social events.

20s and 30s Events: 2008-2009

Bravo Memphis Event – "Sister Myotis"

When: Wed, September 3, 2008, 3pm – 4pm

Where: Voices of the South (map)

Description: An amazing Bravo Memphis event; bring your friends! For more information, visit www.artsmemphis.org/bravo

20s and 30s Kickoff Event – A Sweet Soiree

When: Fri, September 19, 2008, 6:30pm – 9:00pm

Where: ArtsMemphis, 575 S. Mendenhall Road, Memphis, TN (map)

Description: Join us at the exciting Kickoff event for the newly rejuvinated 20s & 30s group, Jews Around Memphis! "Sweet Soiree" at ArtsMemphis No cost! Parking on south end of ArtsMemphis parking lot. Free babysitting for this event, RSVP by Sept. 15 to Celia Mutchnick, 937-2781, celiam@timemphis.org.

20s and 30s – Family Zoo Outing!

When: Sun, September 28, 2008, 9:45am – 11:45am

Where: 2000 Prentiss Place Memphis, TN 38112 (map)

Description: Join Jews Around Memphis for a wonderful wildlife experience! We will meet together at the zoo for an exciting private Zoo encounter at 10:00 AM where we will be introduced to animals and hands-on activities. After the activities, you are free to tour the zoo at your leisure. The cost for the event is $5 per family for Zoo members and $10 per family for non-members. This event is for families with children 5 and under, so please RSVP to rabbiadam@timemphis.org or celiam@timemphis.org

Bravo Memphis Event – Mini-Indie Film Fest

When: Wed, October 1, 2008, 6:30pm – 8:30pm

Where: Indie Memphis (map)

Description: Join Bravo Memphis for the exciting evening. This is a members-only event, so please make sure to purchase your Bravo Memphis memberships. They can be received through the community six-pack or purchased separately through Temple Israel by going to http://www.timemphis.org/about/jam.htm. For more information on Bravo Memphis check out http://about.artsmemphis.com/bravo.

Jews Around Memphis Whiskey Tasting

When: Thu, October 16, 2008, 7pm – 9pm

Where: The Home of Leigh and Craig Royal (map)

Description: Our next event will be a Whiskey (Bourbon) Tasting Thursday, October 16th from 7-9 pm at the home of Leigh and Craig Royal located at 6491 Massey Pointe Cove in Memphis. We will be exploring a variety of bourbons, and the cost of the event will be $10 per person. Refreshments will also be served! Please RSVP to Celia Mutchnick at celiam@timemphis.org or by phone at 937-2781 by October 14th. You can look at a sample the bourbons we might be experiencing at www.greatbourbon. com and www.sazerac.com!

Election Night Political Party

When: Tue, November 4, 2008, 6:30pm – 8:30pm

Where: The home of Rabbi Adam and Amy Grossman, 7262 Cedar Lane, Germantown, TN 38138 (map)

Description: Join Jews Around Memphis as we celebrate U.S. Election Night with friends and family, desserts, and drinks! Babysitting will be available.

Bravo Memphis Event – Fences

When: Tue, November 18, 2008, 6:30pm – 8:30pm

Where: Hattiloo Theatre (map)

Description: Join Bravo Memphis for the exciting evening at the theater. This is a members only event, so please make sure to purchase your Bravo Memphis memberships. They can be received through the community six-pack or purchased separately through Temple Israel by going to http://www.timem-phis.org/about/jam.htm. For more information on Bravo Memphis check out http://about.artsmemphis. com/bravo.

Thanksgiving Fun at Young Avenue Deli

When: Thu, November 27, 2008, 8:30pm – Fri, November 28, 2008, 12:00am

Where: Young Avenue Deli, 2119 Young Avenue, Memphis, TN 38104 (map)

Description: Join Jews Around Memphis for a fun night on the town! Everyone is invited (residents of Memphis and people just in town for the holiday weekend!) as we bring Thanksgiving to a close with fun and friends

Bravo Memphis Event – Nut Remix

When: Fri, December 5, 2008, 6:30pm – 8:30pm

Where: New Ballet Ensemble (map)

Description: Join Bravo Memphis for the exciting evening at the Ballet. This is a members only event, so please make sure to purchase your Bravo Memphis memberships. They can be received through the community six-pack or purchased separately through Temple Israel by going to http://www.timem-phis.org/about/jam.htm. For more information on Bravo Memphis check out http://about.artsmemphis. com/bravo

Latkes and Lights

When: Fri, December 19, 2008, 6pm – 9pm

Where: The Home of Meggan and Daniel Kiel – 1741 Autumn Avenue, Memphis, TN 38112 (map)

Description: A fun Chanukah celebration for both kids and adults! We will meet at the home of Meggan and Daniel Kiel for latkes then at 7:15 leave as a group to see the lights at the Memphis Zoo!

Dreidels and Dim Sum Bash!

When: Wed, December 24, 2008, 7:30pm – 10:30pm

Where: Beauty Shop/Do – 966 S. Cooper Street, Memphis, TN 38104 (map)

Description: Join Jews Around Memphis for a Chanukah night on the town! With dim sum appetizers, drinks, live music, and new friends, this event is sure to be a memorable one! Mark your calendars now!

Thursday Night Kicka$#

When: Thu, January 15, 6:30pm – 8:00pm

Where: Temple Israel – Scheidt Family Center (map)

Description: Join us for a fun night of stress relief while learning some useful self-defense techniques. Tae Kwon Do expert Chris Miller from Cordova Tae Kwon Do will lead a fun class for everyone! Learn about practical defense moves and hang out with friends at this mid-week fun event!

Bravo Memphis Event – urbanArt

When: Thu, January 15, 6:30pm – 8:30pm

Where: urbanArt Commission (map)

Description: Join Bravo Memphis for the exciting evening dedicated to creating a dynamic, vibrant, nurturing community through art and design. This is a members only event, so please make sure to purchase your Bravo Memphis memberships. They can be received through the community six-pack or purchased separately through Temple Israel by going to http://www.timemphis.org/about/jam.htm. For more information on Bravo Memphis check out http://about.artsmemphis.com/bravo.

Bravo Memphis Event – Chinese New Year

When: Tue, February 3, 6:30pm – 8:30pm

Where: Belz Asian and Judaic Museum (map)

Description: Join Bravo Memphis to ring in the Chinese New Year by viewing some of the Belz Museum's wonderful collection. This is a members only event, so please make sure to purchase your Bravo Memphis memberships. They can be received through the community six-pack or purchased separately through Temple Israel by going to http://www.timemphis.org/about/jam.htm. For more information on Bravo Memphis check out http://about.artsmemphis.com/bravo.

Chapter Four College and 20s/30s   **195**

Beer Tasting at Production Brewery

When: Thu, February 5, 6:30pm – 8:00pm

Where: Production Brewery, 827 S. Main Street, Memphis, TN 38106 (map)

Description: Join us as we taste several kinds of beers at Production Brewery for Ghost River Brewing. We will also be taking a tour of the brewery! No cost for the event but be sure to bring some money to purchase a growler of your favorite brew! To RSVP, email celiam@timemphis by Feb. 1st!

Progressive Shabbat Dinner

When: Fri, February 20, 6:30pm – 9:00pm

Where: The Goldbergs, the Lipmans, and the Taubs (map)

Description: A fun night of food and friends – each course at a different home! RSVP (to Adam Grossman at rabbiadam@timemphis.org) by Feb. 16th to insure we have enough food. 6:30 – 7:15 pm First Course/Appetizers: Rachel and Ricki Goldberg 491 McElroy Memphis, TN 38120 7:30 – 8:15 pm Main Course/Entrée: Josh and Joanna Lipman 500 Carysbrook Cove Memphis, TN 38120 8:30 – 9:15 or so Third Course/Dessert: Elyssa and Marc Taub 6371 Garden Oaks Drive Memphis, TN 38120

The Art of Food

When: Fri, March 13, 6:00pm – 8:30pm

Where: Temple Israel, 1376 E. Massey Road, Memphis, TN 38120 (map)

Description: Food, drinks, a VERY special culinary demonstration by Karen Blockman Carrier (owner of Beauty Shop, Do, Mollie Fontaine Lounge, etc), and hands-on food preparation – this night is sure to please the beginning cook to the kitchen expert! Babysitting will be available. Sign up online.

Bravo Memphis Event – Backstage Pass with Awadagin Pratt

When: Fri, March 13, 6:30pm – 8:30pm

Where: Memphis Symphony Orchestra (map)

Description: Join Bravo Memphis at the Symphony for the exciting opportunity to meet Awadagin Pratt. This is a members only event, so please make sure to purchase your Bravo Memphis memberships. They can be received through the community six-pack or purchased separately through Temple Israel by going to http://www.timemphis.org/about/jam.htm. For more information on Bravo Memphis check out http://about.artsmemphis.com/bravo.

Jews Around Memphis goes to Pump It Up!

When: Sun, March 22, 9:30am – 11:00am

Where: Pump It Up in Bartlett, 8000 US Highway 64, Bartlett, TN (map)

Description: A memorable trip to Pump It Up for both kids and adults! Only $5/child. Simply sign up at https://templetest.wufoo.com/forms/pump-it-up-march-22-2009/

Bravo Memphis Event – Faust (Arts Memphis)

When: Thu, April 23, 6:30pm – 8:30pm

Where: Opera Memphis (map)

Description: Join Bravo Memphis for the exciting opportunity to see the opera "Faust." This is a members only event, so please make sure to purchase your Bravo Memphis memberships. They can be received through the community six-pack or purchased separately through Temple Israel by going to http://www.timemphis.org/about/jam.htm. For more information on Bravo Memphis check out http://about.artsmemphis.com/bravo.

Playhouse on the Square – Production of "Third"

When: Sat, May 9, 7:30pm – 10:00pm

Where: Playhouse on the Square – 51 S Cooper, Memphis, TN (map)

Description: Join us for an exclusive performance of "Third" at Playhouse on the Square! Tickets are $12.50 each and are limited, so RSVP by May 1st to rabbiadam@timemphis.org.

Jews Around Memphis go to the Redbirds

When: Sat, June 6, 6:00pm – 8:30pm

Where: Autozone Park (at Second and Union), downtown (map)

Description: Join us for a good time and some good baseball. Redbirds vs. NEW. Game starts at 6:05, tickets are $7/each (kids under 3 are free!) if you RSVP to rabbiadam@timemphis.org by May 29th! Make your reservations today!

Evite:

Dear Jews Around Memphis,

We are writing to invite you to a very exciting event on March 13th, "The Art of Food." We will be having a wonderful food demonstration and hands-on cooking "class" led by Karen Carrier (owner of Beauty Shop, Do, and Molly Fontaine Lounge). Following that, we will all sit down and enjoy our creations at a special Shabbat Dinner. The event details are below, and we hope that you can join us!

To reserve your spot online, all you need to do is visit https://templetest.wufoo.com/forms/the-art-of-food-march-13-2009 by March 10th. Hope to see you all there!

Adam and Celia

What: **Jews Around Memphis**

"The Art of Food"

Hands-on food demo and class by Karen Carrier

and a delicious Shabbat dinner

When: **Friday, March 13th**

6:00 – 8:30 pm

Cost: $10 per person

Where: **Temple Israel Kitchen and East Hall**

1376 East Massey Road

Memphis, TN 38120

RSVP: **To** https://templetest.wufoo.com/forms/the-art-of-food-march-13-2009 **by March 10th.**

Babysitting is available – inquire to Celia (celiam@timemphis.org) by March 10th

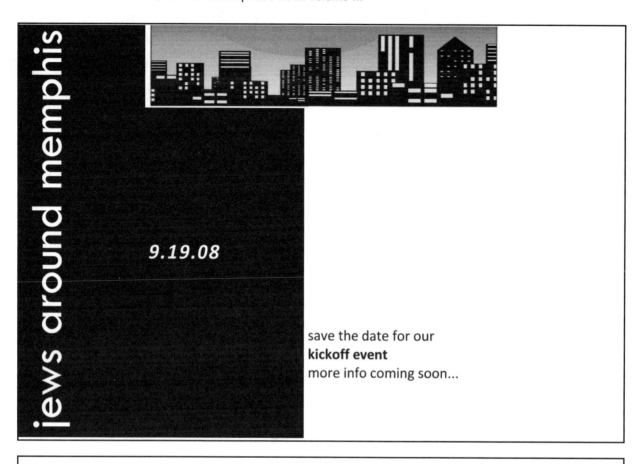

Chapter Four College and 20s/30s **199**

JEWS AROUND MEMPHIS PRESENTS

A Sweet Soiree

KICK OFF THE NEW YEAR IN STYLE
WITH DELICIOUS FOOD, LIVE MUSIC, AND COCKTAILS

Jews Around Memphis is a recently **REJUVENATED** group dedicated to providing 20s and 30s **SINGLES**, **COUPLES**, and **YOUNG FAMILIES** a fun and **FULFILLING** outlet for **JEWISH LIFE**.

FRIDAY, SEPT. 19TH, 2008 6:30–9:00 PM

ARTSMEMPHIS
575 S. MENDENHALL RD.
MEMPHIS, TENNESSEE

PARKING AVAILABLE ON THE SOUTH END OF THE LOT

NO COST FOR THIS EVENT

RSVP: CELIA MUTCHNICK (937.2781 OR CELIAM@TIMEMPHIS.ORG) BY SEPT. 15TH

BE SURE TO ASK ABOUT FREE BABYSITTING

Jews Around Memphis presents....
Dreidels and Dim Sum Bash

December 24th, 2008
7:30–10:30 pm
Dõ/The Beauty Shop
966 S. Cooper / Memphis, TN 38104

* *Delicious Appetizers*
   * *Music by Mojo Possum*
      * *Cash Bar*

This event is free of Charge
RSVP by Dec. 20th to celiam@timemphis.org
Contact us For Babysitting options

Jews Around Memphis
1376 East Massey Road
Memphis, TN 38120

Jews Around Memphis
Dreidels and Dim Sum Raffle

Name: _____

Address: _____

_____

Phone: _____

Email address: _____

Are you new to Memphis? ___ Y ___ N

Are you on our email list? ___ Y ___ N

How did you hear about this event? _____

Must be present to win!

JEWS AROUND MEMPHIS FAMILY OUTING TO THE MEMPHIS ZOO!

Join us for a wonderful wildlife experience! We will meet together at the Zoo for an exciting private Zoo encounter at 9:45 AM where we will be introduced to animals and hands-on activities. After the activities, you are free to tour the zoo at your leisure.

Sunday, September 28th
Cost: $5 per family

9:45—11:45 am at the Memphis Zoo
2000 Prentiss Place Memphis, TN 38112

This event is for families with children 5 and under and space is limited, so please RSVP to rabbiadam@timemphis.org or celiam@timemphis.org by Sept. 24th.

Business Name

Primary Business Address
Your Address Line 2
Your Address Line 3
Your Address Line 4

PLEASE
PLACE
STAMP
HERE

Mailing Address Line 1
Mailing Address Line 2
Mailing Address Line 3
Mailing Address Line 4
Mailing Address Line 5

Chapter Four College and 20s/30s **203**

Gesher *(Bridge)*

Name of Congregation:	Temple Sinai
Address:	5645 Dupree Dr. NW, Atlanta, GA, 30327
Phone Number:	404.252.3073
Contact's Name and E-mail:	blevenberg@templesinaiatlanta.org
Number of Member Units:	1277
URJ District:	South District
Rabbis:	Ronald M. Segal, Bradley G. Levenberg, and Elana E. Perry
Membership Chairperson:	Jaime Gimpelson (chair of our 20s/30s Program)

Brief Description: In the spring of 2007, Temple Sinai embarked on an initiative aimed at attracting unaffiliated Jews in the 20s/30s demographic to the congregation. We are submitting the entirety of our program year for the Belin Outreach and Membership Award.

Program Goal: The Temple Sinai *Gesher* group provides meaningful opportunities to explore Jewish tradition and enrich our Jewish experience. We link young adults in their twenties and thirties to a welcoming, diverse, Reform Jewish community, even if they are not yet members of Temple Sinai. Some programs involve social action, some involve Jewish learning, some involve holiday celebrations. . . . All involve socializing and fun!

Target Population: Unaffiliated Jews in the 20s/30s demographic.

Number of Participants: Some programs are boutique programs with only a handful of participants, other programs reach out to upwards of 150–200 people. Since May 2007, seventy-two member units have joined Temple Sinai as a direct result of these outreach initiatives.

Number and Length of Sessions: There are twelve programs, roughly one per month.

Staffing Required: Our program has succeeded in part because it has never been about attracting large numbers of participants, but rather it is aimed at starting and strengthening relationships within the demographic and between the demographic and the congregation and the rabbis. Thus, at least one rabbi must be present at each program.

Total Cost of Program: $1,500/year.

Source of Funding: The congregation budgeted the funds to support this program.

Fee for Attendees: It is rare for a program cost to be above $20/participant. Of those with a fee, many cost between $5 and $15/person. Most programs are free of charge.

Logistics: Each program required a separate setup. A detailed list follows, broken down by program.

204   The Outreach and Membership Idea Book Volume III

Instructions to Facilitator: The key is about communication. Tech-savvy means of communication are often the most rewarding. The facilitator should plan on showing up early and staying late to each program.

Evaluation of the Program: Our program has been a tremendous success. In addition to engaging seventy-two new members, we have firmly established our programming amongst this demographic as exciting and impressive. Though the programs that involve alcohol have been our largest success in terms of numbers, we can say that hundreds of members of the demographic now have relationships with the Temple Sinai clergy. Even if they have not joined yet, the groundwork has been established to nurture those relationships and welcome them into the fold of Temple Sinai in the years to come.

Logistics Details: There are three key components to our *Gesher* program:

1. Relationships

2. Programming

3. Membership

1. Relationships: The rabbis staffing this program make themselves available to meet with interested parties, either in the evenings after meetings or during the day over lunch. We make sure that each person who reaches out with questions—even the most ordinary—has an invitation to get together for face time. Further, in addition to flyers advertising each program, we reach out directly via phone, e-mail, or Facebook to personally invite participants with whom we have relationships. This has led to an exceptional feeling of connectedness and many of those who have joined the congregation have mentioned these exchanges as selling points.

2. Programming: Our program actually begins over the summer, when we have two outdoor, late-night Shabbat services—one in June and the other in August.

June: Shabbat in the Park(ing lot); services from 8:15 to 9:00, free wine-tasting to follow

August: Shabbat in the Park(ing lot); services from 8:15 to 9:00; free scotch-tasting to follow. These services are held in our scenic Lehrman Garden and draw between thirty and fifty people. Water and soda, as well as fruit and cheese trays, are also provided, free of charge.

September/October: Appletini Bar
Coinciding with Shabbat T'shuvah, 20s/30s join the congregation for the regularly scheduled 6:30–7:30 Shabbat service. Immediately following the service, participants are invited to a separate area of the synagogue to enjoy free Appletinis, Honeytinis, Cosmos, beer, wine, water, and soda. Fruit and chips are also available. This program drew thirty-five people in 2007 and eighty people in 2008. The program cost the congregation $150.

October: Sukkot Program
On the Sunday night during Sukkot, our group partners with the local young adult chapter of the AJC, Access. For a $10 fee, participants can have Mexican food, beer, water, and soda. The entire program takes place in our outdoor courtyard (the location of our congregational Sukkah). There is a formal presentation midway through the evening touting the partnership between our two organizations and offering a teaching on Sukkot. In 2007, the event drew almost 100 people. In 2008, 185 people participated. The program cost the congregation $400.

Chapter Four   College and 20s/30s   **205**

November: Shabbat Program
This program has taken on a very distinct feel each time we have offered it. In 2007, we held a learning session after services. For the session, we had three presenters, each speaking for forty-five minutes to a small group. The group would then rotate (and mix a bit) to one of the other presenters. Thus, each presenter spoke three times to small groups of people. We had a representative from AIPAC, a member of our congregation who spoke about the Torah portion, and a genetic biologist who discussed the ethics of stem cell research. This program drew about eighty people and was a big hit. This program was free and cost the congregation $300 for dinner.

For 2008, we attempted to offer a Shabbat at Home evening, which would pair people with others and invite them to spend a Shabbat dinner together. Sadly, this program suffered from a poor choice of dates and lax PR. Due to lack of interest, we cancelled the program.

December: Theology Café
For this program we partnered with Barnes & Noble to hold a discussion about theology on their premises. The program was well received, though only sparsely attended, and cost us only one cup of coffee for each RSVP.

January: An Evening with Dan Nichols
Temple Sinai brought in Dan Nichols for a Musician in Residence weekend, and we encouraged 20s/30s participants to attend the Saturday night program free of charge. We had over sixty participants from that demographic alone—a huge hit that, due to also inviting our Brotherhood and Sisterhood, allowed bridges to be built between the auxiliaries and cost the *Gesher* group nothing.

February: Mitzvah Day
Originally, we intended to participate in the JFSJ Retreat. However, our members could not commit to a weekend away. Thus, we had a special *Gesher* program on Mitzvah Day, which drew eighteen participants. The community-service draw was one that appealed to our group and we will replicate this program in 2010.

March: Purim
Temple Sinai produces an Adult-Only Purim Shpiel. In 2008, sixteen *Gesher* members attended; so far, in 2009, thirty-eight *Gesher* members are signed up. The program costs $22/person and, since it is a Temple Sinai event, all logistics are handled by other departments within Temple Sinai.

April: Second Night Passover Seder
As Atlanta is a hub for transplants to the south, Temple Sinai is hosting a Second Night Seder for those in our 20s/30s demographic without a home for Seder.

May: *Tikkun Leil Shavuot*
A late-night study session drew thirty-five participants in 2008. Cost was free for participants. The only expenses were for food: $30.

3. Membership: As no Jewish experience is the same, no young person's financial situation is the same. There are many ways one can contribute to the Temple Sinai family. We understand that life is more costly now for members in this demographic, with new expenses ranging from car payments to mortgages to student loans. Thus, we have established a dues structure that is intended to enable young adults to join Temple Sinai without having to give up membership at the gym!

Dues Breakdown:

- Year 1: $180 (or free for children of Sinai Members in this age group)
- Year 2: $250
- Year 3: $400 or 1 percent of your gross annual income (your choice!)

Building Maintenance Fund:

- Only $2,200.00 payable over eight years. Payments do not begin until age 32.
- This structure has made congregational membership a possibility for many singles and couples who previously could not afford the high cost of congregational affiliation.

Conclusion: We are all quite proud of our success and continue to learn from our failures. We do not have the resources to devote a full-time staff position to this outreach initiative, nor can we afford an excessive budget to compete with some of the other communal agencies. What we can offer is an exciting program, an engaging community, and a warm and welcoming environment. If our mission is to lower the obstacles to congregational affiliation, we believe we are succeeding in very real ways.

Welcome
Home...

We're glad you're
here.

Temple Sinai
5645 Dupree Drive
Atlanta, GA 30327
Ph: 404.252.3073
www.templesinaiatlanta.org

Under 32?

Consider
Making
Temple Sinai
YOUR
TEMPLE!

Your Fun

The Temple Sinai Gesher group provides meaningful opportunities to explore Jewish tradition and enrich our Jewish experience. We link young adults in their 20's and 30's to a welcoming, diverse, Reform Jewish community, even if you are not yet a member of Temple Sinai.

Some programs involve social action, some involve Jewish learning, some involve holiday celebrations....
all involve socializing and fun!

Your Trust

As no Jewish experience is the same, no young person's financial situation is the same. There are many ways one can contribute to the Sinai family.

Please contact Steve Bram, Executive Director, at his personal and confidential email address—
sbram@templesinaiatlanta.org
with any questions or concerns you might have.

We have built a temple of 1,200+ members strong, and that allows one to help another.

Chapter Four   College and 20s/30s   **209**

Your Shekels

We understand that life is more costly now, with new expenses ranging from car payments to mortgages.

At Sinai, one family looks after another. That is why it costs only $180. to join Temple Sinai for the first year if you are between the ages of 21 – 32.

Dues Breakdown:
Year 1 – $180.00
(Free for Children of Sinai Members in this age group)
Year 2 – $250.00
Year 3 (continues until age 32) – $400 or 1% of your gross annual income (It's your choice).

Building Maintenance Fund
($2200.00 payable over 8 years)
Does not begin until you reach age 32!

Your Friends

A synagogue is a great place to socialize with other young Jews in a relaxed atmosphere. Bring a buddy along, or come solo, you're always sure to meet someone new.

Your Schedule

Temple Sinai is aware that as working young adults, your schedule is unique.

Friday night Shabbat worship services are offered at two times— 6:30 pm every week, and 8:00 pm twice a month — to better accommodate your schedules and your preferences.

We also offer special Shabbat services designed solely and specifically for our young adults.

Your Jewish connection - on your schedule- - all in the palm of your hand.

Your Voice

At Temple Sinai, your membership is key. If you want to be part of a great community, let yourself in to a great program!

Email Rabbi Brad Levenberg at gesher@templesinaiatlanta.org

You can also join our Facebook page, "Jews in Atlanta 21-32"

Chapter Four   College and 20s/30s   **211**

Your Family

Not only is Temple Sinai a great place for singles *and* couples, but it's a great place to be with your family. If you have kids, or are thinking of having kids, Temple Sinai is the place for you.

We offer free babysitting services every Friday night and our Preschool is one of the best in Atlanta.

October 3: Appletini Bar

October 19: Sukkot Program

November 14: Shabbat Dinners

December 18: Theology Cafe

January 10: Dan Nichols Night

February 5–9:
JFSJ Community Service Trip

February 22: Mitzvah Day

March 10: Purim Celebration

April 9: 2nd Night Seder

May 28: Tikkun Leil Shavuot

While most programs are free, there will be a small charge for non-Sinai members.

Chapter Five

Early Childhood: Connecting Young Families to Preschool and Congregation

The earlier we connect we them, the longer they remain members of our community. There are no truer words about the value of Early Childhood Education and Programming.

Congregation B'nai Israel's Early Childhood Center connected the beauty of Jewish ritual in the home with the value of Jewish synagogue community using **Goodnight Shabbat**. Families in the Early Childhood Center were invited to take turns hosting their preschool child's class for Havdalah, with the rabbi, preschool director, and teachers joining them. The preschool families felt a strong connection to the synagogue as they socialized and bonded, increasing the possibility that they would participate in small *chavurot* and affinity groups. This was also a terrific way to reach out to interfaith families and those who had never observed Havdalah, and introduce the ritual in a comfortable setting.

Little ones love music and sharing experiences with their parents and family. Holy Blossom Temple combined these elements in **Little Blossoms**, a pre-Shabbat music program focused on activity and song for children (0–2 years) and their parents or grandparents. The music portion is led by an early childhood educator who incorporates English and Hebrew, followed by time with the rabbi who shares stories and encourages discussion on various topics. Everyone goes home with a challah for Shabbat. There is time afterwards for play and visiting. Holy Blossom Temple has discovered that Little Blossoms strengthens the connection of multiple generations already affiliated in some way, as well as serving to introduce unaffiliated and interfaith families to the community.

Goodnight Shabbat

Congregation:	Congregation B'nai Israel
Address:	2200 Yamato Road, Boca Raton, FL 33431
Phone number:	561-241-8118
Contact's Name and E-mail:	Rabbi Bloch rabbibloch@cbiboca.org; Linda Harris lharris@cbiboca.org
Number of Member Units:	1150
URJ District:	Southern District
Rabbi:	Rabbi Marci R. Bloch
Membership Chair:	Dana Yormark

Brief Description: Each family in our pre-K is invited to host their child's class and parents for *Havdalah* in their home. On the evening of the program, rabbi, educator, program coordinator, and pre-K teachers arrive at the host's home. Name tags and prayer sheets are distributed to parents as they arrive. The rabbi begins by conducting *Havdalah* with children and parents. She asks that children answer questions and join in *Havdalah* since they participate in this ritual each week at school on Monday mornings. After *Havdalah*, the children and parents are separated in different rooms so that parallel learning can take place. The rabbi and educator work with parents while the program coordinator and pre-K teachers work with children. The children work on craft projects related to *Havdalah* and stories are read to them. Simultaneously, the rabbi and educator teach parents about *Havdalah* and share experiences related to Jewish rituals. The rabbi discusses the importance of making Jewish memories for children and the importance of creating Jewish bedtime rituals. When the programs are completed, the children join their parents. The rabbi leads parents through the Jewish bedtime ritual of reciting the *Sh'ma* and blessing their children. The evening ends with a special hug and everyone greets one another with *shavua tov*.

Program Goals: To build a relationship with the rabbi; to educate families in Jewish rituals; to illustrate the importance of Jewish memories; to connect and build a relationship with the religious school and its director; to foster parents' desire to support and participate in their child's Jewish education; to retain our preschool families as synagogue members and/or to help them affiliate for the first time; to reach out to interfaith families in a comfortable setting; to help create friendships; and finally, to promote bonding among families, increasing the possibility that they will participate in small *chavurot* and affinity groups.

Target Population: Parents of our pre-K students, including interfaith couples, members, and non-member families.

Staffing Required: Rabbi, educator, program coordinator and 3 pre-K teachers.

Total Cost of Program: $375.00 per session (including supplies and staff). Total cost for all sessions was $2,625.00.

Chapter Five   Early Childhood   **215**

Source of Funding: Congregation B'nai Israel Parent Organization.

Fees for attendees: Free.

Logistics: The date of each class's Goodnight Shabbat program is listed on the school calendar at the beginning of each year. Parents volunteer with the program coordinator to be a host family for the program. The program coordinator sends a letter to the host family outlining the evening, explaining what needs to be purchased. Parents then receive an invitation from the school approximately one month in advance of the assigned date of the program. In addition, host parents make individual calls to each family in the class.

Each host family's home must have two large rooms and/or an outside space for parallel learning. The host family is asked to purchase pizza, drinks, dessert, and paper goods. Following the program, the preschool reimburses the host family for all their costs. *Havdalah* set, wine, prayer sheets, craft project for children, and stories are supplied by the program coordinator. The program coordinator and three pre-K teachers are needed to facilitate the children's crafts. A rabbi and educator are needed to facilitate the parents' class.

Evaluation of Program: Every Goodnight Shabbat program has an attendance of 80 percent. The evaluation is done orally and feedback is given to teachers and preschool director. The reputation of this program is known throughout the preschool.

Follow-up: Thank-you notes are sent to all host families by the rabbi and early childhood director. Follow-up letters are sent by the rabbi to all participants thanking them for attending and letting them know of her availability.

216 The Outreach and Membership Idea Book Volume III

Goodnight Shabbat Program
Outline for Session

4:45-5:00pm	Preparation for Program
5:00-5:20pm	*Havdalah* with Families
5:20-5:45pm	Parallel Learning

    a) Rabbi teaches parents about Jewish Rituals

    b) Program Coordinator with assistance of Pre-K teachers leads crafts and stories with children.

5:45-6:00pm	Rabbi leads families in Jewish Bedtime Rituals
6:00-7:00pm	Families share in dinner and dessert

4:45-5:00pm Preparation for Program
Program Coordinator arrives and distributes name tags to parents and children and organizes with host parents. Rabbi and Educator arrive shortly thereafter and greet families.

5:00-5:20pm Havdalah with Families
1) Rabbi greets all families and asks them to greet one another. Rabbi then explains Goodnight Shabbat and purpose of the program. She then outlines what will happen during the evening to explain to parents and children what will occur.

2) Rabbi, with Educator, Program Coordinator, Pre-K teachers and families, conduct *Havdalah* together. Rabbi asks children about the symbols involved in the *Havdalah* ceremony and teaches about this ritual. After conclusion of *Havdalah*, everyone wishes one another *Shavua Tov*.

3) Rabbi explains that they will now separate for parallel learning.

5:20-5:45pm Parallel Learning

A) Rabbi Teaches about Jewish Bedtime Rituals
 1) After parents and children separate, Rabbi teaches adults more about *Havdalah* and talks about the importance of Jewish rituals to families in general. She and the Educator ask the parents to share their names and a Jewish ritual object that is special in their home or was in their home when growing up.

 2) Rabbi then speaks about the importance of rituals and creating memories with families. Rabbi and Educator share their own personal stories of Jewish ritual items in their homes and their own Jewish memories. Both share stories about Bedtime *Shema*.

 3) Rabbi then teaches about the importance of creating rituals with their children. She teaches them how to recite the Bedtime *Shema,* and discusses the ritual of blessing children on Friday night.

B) **Program Coordinator** *with assistance of Pre-k teachers leads crafts and stories with children.*

 1) Program Coordinator leads children in crafts. They make *Havdalah* sets and color picture of ritual objects. When children are done, the Program Coordinator reads them stories related to *Havdalah* and/or *Shabbat.*

5:45-6:00pm Rabbi leads families in Jewish Bedtime Rituals

After Rabbi and Educator finish lesson with parents, Rabbi explains that their children will be returning with a craft project and then they will share in closing rituals together.

Children return to the room where parents are and Rabbi asks the children about their project. Children present and share with their parents about what they did. Rabbi then explains to the children what their parents learned. Rabbi asks all children to go to their parents. We discuss how saying the *Shema* is the last thing we do as Jews when we say Goodnight. Everyone joins in saying *Shema*. Rabbi gives parents an opportunity to bless their children. Rabbi asks parents to tell their child a special secret. The evening ends with kisses, hugs and "I love yous" and everyone wishes one another a *Shavua tov.*

6:00-7:00pm Families share in dinner and dessert.

Chapter Five　Early Childhood　**217**

HAVDALAH

with

Families

Rabbi and Educator teach parents about Jewish Rituals.

Programming Coordinator with assistance of Pre-K teachers leads crafts and stories with children.

Rabbi leads families in Jewish Rituals.

A page from the Preschool 2008/2009 calendar showing Goodnight Shabbat on November 1, 2008.

An excerpt from our synagogue newsletter: SHELANU dated November 2008

Nadel Center For
Early Childhood Education
Goodnight Shabbat
Saturday, November 1:
Join **Rabbi Marci R. Bloch** for a hands-on *Havdalah* service in a classmate's home. Dress your children in their favorite PJs and bring a hearty appetite as we come together for dinner and schmoozing. Rabbi Bloch will lead a light discussion about making Jewish memories with your children and incorporating Jewish rituals in your home. An art activity will be led by **Miss Debbie.** *Each Pre-K class will have their own Goodnight Shabbat on a specific date. You will be notified when your Goodnight Shabbat program will be.*

"GOODNIGHT SHABBAT"

WITH RABBI MARCI R. BLOCH

Pre-K Havdalah Service
for families in Room 102
Saturday, November 1, 2008
5:00-7:00 pm

> At the home of Cindy and Gregg Jaffy
> Directions will follow.

Highlights of the Evening:
Dinner, Havdalah Service, Cookies and Milk
Jewish Bedtime Rituals and Story
Have the children bring their favorite Teddy Bear!

Please RSVP to Debbie in the school office. 241-1484 or email
debbie@cbiboca.org

A sample thank you letter to a host family.

CONGREGATION
B'NAI ISRAEL

February 16, 2009
22 Shevat, 5769

Mr. & Mrs. Marc Wites
17625 Middlebrook Way
Boca Raton, FL 33496

Dear Jennifer & Marc,

Thank you so much for hosting our preschool program "Goodnight Shabbat." It was so kind of you both to open your home for this very special experience of learning and fun. It was clear to us from the attendance of children and their parents that this type of program is highly valued.

We look forward to sharing many other special programs with you and creating new connections for you within our preschool and in our synagogue.

Again thank you for everything. We are blessed to have people like you in our CBI family.

With prayers for blessings,

Marci R. Bloch   Linda Harris
Rabbi   NCECE Preschool Director

A sample thank you letter to a participating family.

CONGREGATION
B'NAI ISRAEL

February 23, 2009
29 Shevat, 5769

Dr. & Mrs. Michael Shore
5700 Nassau Dr
Boca Raton, FL 33487

Dear Melissa & Michael,

It was such a wonderful joy to be with you Saturday night, February 7th. I hope observing *Havdalah* and learning with you and your children was as much fun for you as it was for me. I also hope that our conversation may have helped you to begin thinking about creating Jewish rituals and memories with your family. I look forward to many more opportunities to worship and learn together again in the future.

Please know that if you need anything at all, I am here for you. Please feel free to contact me at rabbibloch@cbiboca.org or 561-241-8118.

With prayers for blessings,

Rabbi Marci R. Bloch

A letter to Rabbi from a classroom and teachers.

February 9, 2009

Dear Rabbi Marci

Thank you for a lovely Goodnight Shabbat. The children and teachers as well as the parents had a marvelous time. We learned and had a warm feeling as we got to cuddle with our loved ones as we said goodbye to Shabbat for another week. It was very nice to share this intimate experience with you. You made it feel so special! We hope that our mommies and daddies spend more time experiencing the Judaism part of our curriculum with us as we continue to learn and grow as young Jewish boys and girls entering into many different schools for Kindergarten. We are thrilled that we had this time to share with them and with you.

With much love and appreciation,

The teachers and children of 101

JENNY SILBERFARB
9411 GRAND ESTATES WAY
BOCA RATON, FLORIDA 33496

December 8, 2008

Rabbi Marci Bloch
Congregation B'nai Israel
2200 Yamato Road
Boca Raton, Florida 33431

Dear Rabbi Bloch,

I just wanted to thank you for coming into my home and sharing such a wonderful Shabbat with Susie and her friends from Room 104. **Goodnight Shabbat** is such a wonderful program- I was so thrilled to host it in my home. It is such a special time for these very impressionable children. In our house, we really try to uphold the traditions of Shabbat and having you, our Rabbi, here to close Shabbat for the week, was so special.

Thanks again and I look forward to housing it again for Joey when he gets to Pre-K.

xoxo

Jenny

Jenny Silberfarb

Little Blossoms

Congregation: Holy Blossom Temple

Address: 1950 Bathurst Street, Toronto, Ontario

Phone number: 416-789-3291

Contact's Name and E-mail: stramer@holyblossom.org

Number of Member Units: 2100

URJ District: Canada

Rabbis: John Moscowitz, Yael Splansky, Karen Thomashow

Membership Chair: Joan Garson

Brief Description: Little Blossoms is a pre-Shabbat music program for parents or grandparents and children (0–2 years) with focused activity and song. It is led by an early childhood educator who incorporates English and Hebrew in her high-energy, very interesting program. Our rabbis visit the group at the end of the music portion and share stories and encourage discussion on various topics. Everyone goes home with a challah for Shabbat. There is time afterwards for play and visiting.

Program Goals: To attract and connect young moms/dads to the temple; to reconnect our members and provide them with a program to which they can bring their young grandchildren; to provide a missing and clearly much-needed program that offers a way to begin to feel comfortable at the temple for young members who have married our members and are new to the temple, as well as unaffiliated young people in the neighborhood. We have seen, in many ways, how those who attend programs here, even as nonmembers, eventually, and quite naturally, begin to see the temple as their home. And ultimately, when they feel the time is right to join a congregation, there is no question for them about joining HBT.

Target Population: Our target population was young adults, prospective members, and older members, as well as new members and all young families in our neighborhood.

Number of Participants: Two classes are run each session. Total approximately forty adults and forty infants and toddlers.

Number and Length of Sessions: We are currently running our third eight-week session. We have a waiting list for future sessions.

Staffing Required: One temple staff person to organize and process registration. Facilities personnel to set up the room. Outside program leader with experience in music and early childhood education.

Total Cost of Program: $2,900 per session.

Source of Funding: Self-funded.

Fee for Attendees: $115 for members, $130 for nonmembers.

Logistics: Large space with carpet; pillows, coffee, tea, muffins, toys. Try to create an intimate and comfortable environment.

Instructions to Facilitator: To create an interactive, high-energy, inclusive and joyous program. To help provide a comfortable environment and encourage interaction between the participants. To create a place where the participants feel welcomed and have the desire to linger after the program is done.

Evaluation of Program: Overwhelming success. Prospective members translating into members, older members and longtime members feeling reconnected to the temple and to other members. Young adult members attending programs (aside from High Holy Days) for the first time and finding their own place at the temple. This program is attended by many nonmembers as well as many young adults who had grown up as members at the temple with their families, and were even married here, but had not been involved in the temple in the past few years. We can already see how offering this program is just what they needed to feel connected with the synagogue once again. To find their own place here, not as part of their parents' membership, but a place that is right for them. We also have a few attending who had called to inquire about membership, but were not yet ready to join.

Follow-up: Each session brings new people and names to add to our mailing lists, which allows us to keep in contact with them, providing membership information and program advertising. All this feedback helps the temple continue to create programs that will reflect the needs and wants of our members and potential members.

Chapter Five Early Childhood 227

little blossoms grow
AT HOLY BLOSSOM TEMPLE

All babies eighteen months and younger are welcome to bring a parent or grandparent for a terrific morning of learning and fun. *Little Blossoms* gives busy babies maximum flexibility to come and go as their schedule allows and offers a variety of programs to meet their many needs and interests. Each Thursday morning will follow the same format with a variety of programming.

9:30 - 9:45 am - *sip, snack, & shmooze*

9:45 - 10:30 am - *program time*

10:30 - 11:30 am - *walk, talk & roll* around the neighbourhood or *stay & play* indoors with comfy beanbag seating, toys and books.

To register, please contact Shannon at the Holy Blossom Temple office: 416.789.3291 ext 227

$120 for Temple members
$130 for non-members

Holy Blossom is centrally located at 1950 Bathurst Street, one block south of Eglinton Avenue.

Invite a friend.

Autumn 2008 Program Schedule

October 23
  An Introduction to Baby Sign Language

October 30
  Music & Storytelling with Judy Gershon

November 6
  Make your own organic baby-friendly foods with Daliah Organ

November 13
  Yoga with Michelle Katz

November 20
  Nurturing your Baby's Neshama with Rabbi Yael Splansky

November 27
  Baby CPR and Safety with a trained Instructor

December 4
  Music & storytelling with Judy Gershon

December 11
  Yoga with Michelle Katz

little blossoms
SHABBAT PREP
AT HOLY BLOSSOM TEMPLE

All babies two years old and younger are welcome to bring a parent or grandparent for a terrific morning of pre-*Shabbat* fun. Simone Mayer leads this weekly program of music, singing, movement, stories and snacks. And each week, participants take home a fresh *challah* for their *own Shabbat* tables.

Little Blossoms will run for 8 weeks
on Friday mornings,
March 27, - May 15, 2009.
Two age appropriate timeslots.
10:00 a.m. - 11:00 a.m. for ages 1-2 years
11:00 a.m. - 12:00 p.m. for newborns - 12 months

To register please contact Shannon at the Holy Blossom Temple office:
416.789.3291 ext 227

$115 for Temple members
$130 for non-members

Holy Blossom is centrally located at 1950 Bathurst Street, one block south of Eglinton Avenue.

Invite a friend.

HOLY BLOSSOM TEMPLE
ק"ק פרחי קדש

Simone brings more than 20 years experience as an E.C.E. & Primary school Hebrew teacher to our Shabbat focused program. She encourages both participation & song suggestions from the adults and hopes to create a musical extravaganza for all.
We welcome her to the Holy Blossom community.

Family Programming 2009

Tot Shabbat
Fridays at 6 p.m.
Mark your calendars for our March/April dates: Mar. 6 (Service and dinner) and 20 (Service and craft), and Apr. 3 (Service and dinner) and 17 (Service and craft).

Shabbat Morning Family Services
Mar. 7, 21 and 28, and Apr. 4, 18 and 25
This come-as-you-are Service is a family-friendly, informal way to celebrate Shabbat. Children and teens help to lead the Service. Children's programming, including music, storytelling and creative learning, are integrated throughout the morning. A simple kiddush lunch follows.

Little Blossoms Shabbat Prep — Music with Simone
Fridays at 10 a.m. for children 12 months to two years of age; 11 a.m. for children up to 12 months
Mar. 27 to May 15
This eight-week program is for parents or grandparents and children younger than two years of age. Join Simone Mayer for singalongs, story time and interactive fun. Everyone will go home with his or her very own challah. To register, please call Shannon Tramer (ext. 227), at the Temple.

Ella Berenbaum holds her challah.

Holiday Cooking Workshop: Pesach — Your Seder Table
Sun. Apr. 5, at 12.30p.m.
Join Dalia Organ, from the Academy of Artisans, in the Holy Blossom Temple kitchen, for this special program to plan your seder table. All food is dairy and organic and ingredients are kosher-for-Passover, but the kitchen is not. *Cost: $22 members; $25 non-members.* To register, please call Elana Fehler (ext. 221), at the Temple, or email efehler@holyblossom.org.

For more details on Family Programming events, please see page 1, or call call our hotline (ext. 518), at the Temple.

Seniors' Programming 2009 at HOLY BLOSSOM

MONDAYS
@ the Temple

Do not let the children have all the fun. We invite all seniors to our annual Purim party on Mon. Mar. 9, where we will laugh together as we read our own version of the Megillah, dress up in ridiculous costumes and play games.

Our other upcoming programs include:

Mar. 16 What Did They Learn from Us — Part 2 | **Leo Baeck Day School Students**

Mar. 23 Jews and Repairing the World | **Avrum Rosenzeig**, *Founder, Ve'ahavta, the Canadian Jewish Humanitarian and Relief Committee*

Mar. 30 What Is the Real Cause of Anti-Semitism? | **Rabbi Michael Stroh**

Apr. 6 Moving Scenes: Vignettes about Aging | **Ryerson University's Act II Studio**

WEDNESDAYS
@ the Movies

Mar. 25, at 1 p.m
Richard Rogers
Join us for a documentary film on the well-known composer.

Apr. 29 at 1 p.m.
Almonds and Raisins
This documentary examines the dozens of Yiddish-language films made in the United States and Europe between the release of *The Jazz Singer* in 1927 and the outbreak of the Second World War in 1939. *Cost: $1.*

For more information or to inquire about our transportation project, please leave your name on our Seniors' hotline (ext. 517), at the Temple.